O9-BHJ-859

CHICAGO PUBLIC LIBRARY

R02084 71956

		DATE DUE	

THE CHICAGO PUBLIC LIBRARY

ORIOLE PARK BRANCH
7454 W. BALMORAL
CHICAGO, IL 60656

Bloom's BioCritiques

Dante Alighieri
Maya Angelou
Jane Austen
The Brontë Sisters
Lord Byron
Albert Camus
Geoffrey Chaucer
Anton Chekhov
Joseph Conrad
Stephen Crane
Charles Dickens
Emily Dickinson
T. S. Eliot
Ralph Ellison
William Faulkner
F. Scott Fitzgerald
Robert Frost
Nathaniel Hawthorne
Ernest Hemingway
Langston Hughes
Zora Neale Hurston
James Joyce
Stephen King
Arthur Miller
John Milton
Toni Morrison
Edgar Allan Poe
J. D. Salinger
William Shakespeare
John Steinbeck
Henry David Thoreau
Mark Twain
Alice Walker
Walt Whitman
Tennessee Williams
William Wordsworth

Bloom's BioCritiques

JAMES JOYCE

Edited and with an introduction by
Harold Bloom
Sterling Professor of the Humanities
Yale University

CHELSEA HOUSE
PUBLISHERS
A Haights Cross Communications Company

Philadelphia

©2003 by Chelsea House Publishers, a subsidiary of
Haights Cross Communications.

A Haights Cross Communications ✦ Company

Introduction © 2003 by Harold Bloom.

All rights reserved. No part of this publication may be
reproduced or transmitted in any form or by any means
without the written permission of the publisher.

Printed and bound in the United States of America.

10 9 8 7 6 5 4 3 2 1

Library of Congress Cataloging-in-Publication Data
James Joyce / edited and with an introduction by Harold Bloom.
        p. cm. -- (Bloom's biocritiques)
Includes bibliographical references (p.) and index.
    ISBN 0-7910-7382-3
  1. Joyce, James, 1882–1941--Criticism and interpretation. 2. Ireland-
in literature. I. Bloom, Harold. II. Series.
  PR6019.09Z6335 2003
  823'.912--dc21

                                        2003000805

Chelsea House Publishers
1974 Sproul Road, Suite 400
Broomall, PA 19008-0914

http://www.chelseahouse.com

Contributing editor: Susan V. Scaff

Cover design by Keith Trego

Cover: © Hulton Archive/Getty Images

Layout by EJB Publishing Services

R0208471956

CONTENTS

Oriole Park Branch
7454 W. Balmoral Ave.
Chicago, IL 60656

USER'S GUIDE

These volumes are designed to introduce the reader to the life and work of the world's literary masters. Each volume begins with Harold Bloom's essay "The Work in the Writer" and a volume-specific introduction also written by Professor Bloom. Following these unique introductions is an engaging biography that discusses the major life events and important literary accomplishments of the author under consideration.

Furthermore, each volume includes an original critique that not only traces the themes, symbols, and ideas apparent in the author's works, but strives to put those works into a cultural and historical perspective. In addition to the original critique is a brief selection of significant critical essays previously published on the author and his or her works followed by a concise and informative chronology of the writer's life. Finally, each volume concludes with a bibliography of the writer's works, a list of additional readings, and an index of important themes and ideas.

HAROLD BLOOM

The Work in the Writer

Literary biography found its masterpiece in James Boswell's *Life of Samuel Johnson*. Boswell, when he treated Johnson's writings, implicitly commented upon Johnson as found in his work, even as in the great critic's life. Modern instances of literary biography, such as Richard Ellmann's lives of W. B. Yeats, James Joyce, and Oscar Wilde, essentially follow in Boswell's pattern.

That the writer somehow is in the work, we need not doubt, though with William Shakespeare, writer-of-writers, we almost always need to rely upon pure surmise. The exquisite rancidities of the Problem Plays or Dark Comedies seem to express an extraordinary estrangement of Shakespeare from himself. When we read or attend *Troilus and Cressida* and *Measure for Measure*, we may be startled by particular speeches of Ulysses in the first play, or of Vincentio in the second. These speeches, of Ulysses upon hierarchy or upon time, or of Duke Vincentio upon death, are too strong either for their contexts or for the characters of their speakers. The same phenomenon occurs with Parolles, the military impostor of *All's Well That Ends Well*. Utterly disgraced, he nevertheless affirms: "Simply the thing I am/Shall make me live."

In Shakespeare, more even than in his peers, Dante and Cervantes, meaning always starts itself again through excess or overflow. The strongest of Shakespeare's creatures—Falstaff, Hamlet, Iago, Lear, Cleopatra—have an exuberance that is fiercer than their plays can contain. If Ben Jonson was at all correct in his complaint that "Shakespeare wanted art," it could have been only in a sense that he may not have intended. Where do the personalities of Falstaff or Hamlet touch a limit? What was it in Shakespeare that made the two parts of *Henry IV* and *Hamlet* into "plays unlimited"? Neither Falstaff nor Hamlet will be stopped: their wit, their beautiful, laughing speech, their intensity of being—all these are virtually infinite.

In what ways do Falstaff and Hamlet manifest the writer in the work? Evidently, we can never know, or know enough to answer with any authority. But what would happen if we reversed the question, and asked: How did the work form the writer, Shakespeare?

Of Shakespeare's inwardness, his biography tells us nothing. And yet, to an astonishing extent, Shakespeare created our inwardness. At the least, we can speculate that Shakespeare so lived his life as to conceal the depths of his nature, particularly as he rather prematurely aged. We do not have Shakespeare on Shakespeare, as any good reader of the Sonnets comes to realize: they do not constitute a key that unlocks his heart. No sequence of sonnets could be less confessional or more powerfully detached from the poet's self.

The German poet and universal genius, Goethe, affords a superb contrast to Shakespeare. Of Goethe's life, we know more than everything; I wonder sometimes if we know as much about Napoleon or Freud or any other human being who ever has lived, as we know about Goethe. Everywhere, we can find Goethe in his work, so much so that Goethe seems to crowd the writing out, just as Byron and Oscar Wilde seem to usurp their own literary accomplishments. Goethe, cunning beyond measure, nevertheless invested a rival exuberance in his greatest works that could match his personal charisma. The sublime outrageousness of the Second Part of *Faust*, or of the greater lyric and meditative poems, form a Counter-Sublime to Goethe's own daemonic intensity.

Goethe was fascinated by the daemonic in himself; we can doubt that Shakespeare had any such interests. Evidently, Shakespeare abandoned his acting career just before he composed *Measure for Measure* and *Othello*. I surmise that the egregious interventions by Vincentio and Iago displace the actor's energies into a new kind of mischief-making, a fresh opening to a subtler playwriting-within-the-play.

But what had opened Shakespeare to this new awareness? The answer is the work in the writer, *Hamlet* in Shakespeare. One can go further: it was not so much the play, *Hamlet*, as the character Hamlet, who changed Shakespeare's art forever.

Hamlet's personality is so large and varied that it rivals Goethe's own. Ironically Goethe's Faust, his Hamlet, has no personality at all, and is as colorless as Shakespeare himself seems to have chosen to be. Yet nothing could be more colorful than the Second Part of *Faust*, which is peopled by an astonishing array of monsters, grotesque devils, and classical ghosts.

A contrast between Shakespeare and Goethe demonstrates that in each—but in very different ways—we can better find the work in the person, than we can discover that banal entity, the person in the work. Goethe to many of his contemporaries, seemed to be a mortal god. Shakespeare, so far as we know, seemed an affable, rather ordinary fellow, who aged early and became somewhat withdrawn. Yet Faust, though Mephistopheles battles for his soul, is hardly worth the trouble unless you take him as an idea and not as a person. Hamlet is nearly every-idea-in-one, but he is precisely a personality and a person.

Would Hamlet be so astonishingly persuasive if his father's ghost did not haunt him? Falstaff is more alive than Prince Hal, who says that the devil haunts him in the shape of an old fat man. Three years before composing the final *Hamlet*, Shakespeare invented Falstaff, who then never ceased to haunt his creator. Falstaff and Hamlet may be said to best represent the work in the writer, because their influence upon Shakespeare was prodigious. W. H. Auden accurately observed that Falstaff possesses infinite energy: never tired, never bored, and absolutely both witty and happy until Hal's rejection destroys him. Hamlet too has infinite energy, but in him it is more curse than blessing.

Falstaff and Hamlet can be said to occupy the roles in Shakespeare's invented world that Sancho Panza and Don Quixote possess in Cervantes's. Shakespeare's plays from 1610 on (starting with *Twelfth Night*) are thus analogous to the Second Part of Cervantes's epic novel. Sancho and the Don overtly jostle Cervantes for authorship in the Second Part, even as Cervantes battles against the impostor who has pirated a continuation of his work. As a dramatist, Shakespeare manifests the work in the writer more indirectly. Falstaff's prose genius is revived in the scapegoating of Malvolio by Maria and Sir Toby Belch, while Falstaff's darker insights are developed by Feste's melancholic wit. Hamlet's intellectual resourcefulness, already deadly, becomes poisonous in Iago and in Edmund. Yet we have not crossed into the deeper abysses of the work in the writer in later Shakespeare.

No fictive character, before or since, is Falstaff's equal in self-trust. Sir John, whose delight in himself is contagious, has total confidence both in his self-awareness and in the resources of his language. Hamlet, whose self is as strong, and whose language is as copious, nevertheless distrusts both the self and language. Later Shakespeare is, as it were, much under the influence both of Falstaff and of Hamlet, but they tug him in opposite directions. Shakespeare's own copiousness of language is well-nigh incredible: a vocabulary in excess of twenty-one thousand words, almost eighteen hundred of which he coined himself. And of his word-hoard, nearly half are used only once each, as though the perfect setting for each had been found, and need not be repeated. Love for language and faith in language are Falstaffian attributes. Hamlet will darken both that love and that faith in Shakespeare, and perhaps the Sonnets can best be read as Falstaff and Hamlet counterpointing against one another.

Can we surmise how aware Shakespeare was of Falstaff and Hamlet, once they had played themselves into existence? *Henry IV, Part I* appeared in six quarto editions during Shakespeare's lifetime; *Hamlet* possibly had four. Falstaff and Hamlet were played again and again at the Globe, but Shakespeare knew also that they were being read, and he must have had contact with some of those readers. What would it have been like to discuss Falstaff or Hamlet with one of their early readers (presumably also part of their audience at the Globe), if you were the creator of such demiurges? The question would seem nonsensical to most Shakespeare scholars, but then these days they tend to be either ideologues or moldy figs. How can we recover the uncanniness of Falstaff and of Hamlet, when they now have become so familiar?

A writer's influence upon himself is an unexplored problem in criticism, but such an influence is never free from anxieties. The biocritical problem (which this series attempts to explore) can be divided into two areas, difficult to disengage fully. Accomplished works affect the author's life, and also affect her subsequent writings. It is simpler for me to surmise the effect of *Mrs. Dalloway* and *To the Lighthouse* upon Woolf's late *Between the Acts*, than it is to relate Clarissa Dalloway's suicide and Lily Briscoe's capable endurance in art to the tragic death and complex life of Virginia Woolf.

There are writers whose lives were so vivid that they seem sometimes to obscure the literary achievement: Byron, Wilde, Malraux, Hemingway. But most major Western writers do not live that exuberantly, and the greatest of all, Shakespeare, sometimes appears to have adopted the personal mask of colorlessness. And yet there are heroes of literature who struggled titanically with their own eras— Tolstoy, Milton, Victor Hugo—who nevertheless matter more for their works than their lives.

There are great figures—Emily Dickinson, Wallace Stevens, Willa Cather—who seem to have had so little of the full intensity of life when compared to the vitality of their work, that we might almost speak of the work in the work, rather than even of the work in a person. Emily Brontë might well be the extreme instance of such a visionary, surpassing William Blake in that one regard.

I conclude this general introduction to a series of literary bio-critiques by stating a tentative formula or principle for gauging the many ways in which the work influences the person and her subsequent, later work. Our influence upon ourselves is always related to the Shakespearean invention of self-overhearing, which I have written about in several other contexts. Life, as well as poetry and prose, is overheard rather than simply heard. The writer listens to herself as though she were somebody else, and the will to change begins to operate. The forces that live in us include the prior work we have done, and the dreams and waking visions that evade our dismissals.

HAROLD BLOOM

Introduction

How do you chronicle the principal dates in the life of the premier writer in English of the twentieth century? Dublin's James Joyce might have mentioned February 2, 1882, when he was born, or June 16, 1904, when he took his first walk with Nora Barnacle, a date that became "Bloomsday," when all of *Ulysses* is enacted. Doubtless, he would have added July 26, 1907, when their daughter Lucia was born, and the earlier birth of their son, Giorgio on July 27, 1905. We must record Joyce's death on January 13, 1941, not yet fifty-nine, and the death of Nora Barnacle Joyce on April 10, 1951.

From a reader's perspective, the crucial dates are the publication of Joyce's major works: *Dubliners* (1914), *A Portrait of the Artist as a Young Man* (1916), *Ulysses* (1922), *Finnegans Wake* (1939). No narrative prose fiction in English since Charles Dickens could be judged to equal that sequence in aesthetic eminence, though partisans of Henry James might dispute the point, I suppose. I myself would turn to Dante and to Shakespeare as Joyce's true precursors, and masters. Certainly only they, Cervantes, and Chaucer transcend Joyce in the arts of representation. Blind Milton and Jonathan Swift might be brought forward also, but no others, I think, in English.

Only the authentic though mostly surface difficulties of *Finnegans Wake*, which have prevented a general readership, pragmatically result in the solitary eminence of *Ulysses* among all writings in English, possibly since the seventeenth century. How can we describe the influence of

1

Ulysses upon James Joyce himself, except to say that, to surpass himself, Joyce had to compose *Finnegans Wake*.

Samuel Beckett, writing about *Work in Progress* a decade before it was published as *Finnegans Wake*, charmingly compared the earthly paradises of Dante and Joyce:

> Dante's Terrestrial Paradise is the carriage entrance to a
> Paradise that is not celestial: Mr. Joyce's Terrestrial Paradise
> is the tradesmen's entrance on to the sea-shore.

Beckett, who began as Joyce's most eminent disciple, favors neither Dante nor Joyce over the other. *Ulysses* is too comprehensive to be primarily an *Inferno*, and the *Wake* is too cheerful to be a *Purgatorio*. Had Joyce lived, his old age would have been given to an epic on the sea, presumably not a *Paradiso*.

Mary T. Reynolds, writing about Joyce and Dante, wisely remarked that: "Art, for Joyce, is fatherhood." Leopold Bloom's son, Rudy, is dead, and Stephen, whatever the scheme of *Ulysses*, is not an apt substitute. Fatherhood, in Joyce and in Shakespeare, is a mystery: the image of cuckoldry haunts both. Shakespeare wisely gives us not the slightest clue whether he himself personally was Catholic, Protestant, skeptic, nihilist, or Hermetist. Joyce, we need not doubt, was a *totally* lapsed Catholic. For Joyce, God is a hangman, as he is in Jose Saramago's *The Gospel According to Jesus Christ*. I bring this forward only to point out that "God the Father" is the least Joycean of all possible phrases.

I propose instead: *Ulysses* the father, which returns us to the fatherhood of the marvelous Poldy Bloom. Poldy is Joyce, Shakespeare, and a God purged of the hangman's stigma. That also makes Poldy the Ghost in *Hamlet*, and we should remember that Stephen quotes the subtle Sabellian heresy that the Father was Himself His Own Son.

The effect of Joyce's masterworks upon his own life was uncanny: *Ulysses* and the *Wake* reject Dante's attempt to reconcile poetry and religion. In turn, they rendered Joyce yet more himself. More than any other modern writer, Joyce fathered himself through his own work.

BRETT FOSTER

Biography of James Joyce

"I SHALL TRY MYSELF AGAINST
THE POWERS OF THE WORLD."

Embarking "alone and friendless," a precocious 20-year-old named James Augustine Joyce decided in November 1902 to escape his hometown of Dublin for the promise and fortune of Europe's foremost metropolis, Paris. In this city the author would later in life finish his masterpiece *Ulysses* and compose his great final work, *Finnegans Wake*, but Joyce was about to undertake his first "exile" from Ireland for the most uncharacteristic of reasons: he wished to study medicine at the Sorbonne, France's premiere university.

A recent graduate of the Royal College, Joyce had already grown tired of his Dublin medical training after a mere month of course work, and perhaps he knew even then that his proposed Paris education was merely a pretense, an "official" plan to justify a trip that seemed rash to friends and family, a "hopeless quest," one concerned older writer advised him. Joyce nevertheless felt Paris life would permit him precious time to continue his writing, and in truth he had very little to lose: "I do not know what will happen to me in Paris but my case can hardly be worse than it is here," he wrote Lady Augusta Gregory, an aristocratic patroness of young writers from whom Joyce was seeking financial assistance and contacts.

Joyce's "case" no doubt involved the continuing deterioration of his once-genteel family's social and economic standing. In October,

Joyce's father foolishly cashed in half of his pension (which wasn't large in the first place) in order to purchase a house. His decision would only further the Joyces' financial woes, and he would take out four mortgages on the property within a year. Consequently, no funds were available to pay Joyce's medical school expenses. He had hoped to find work as a tutor, but none was forthcoming, and he quickly inferred from this failure that Dublin's college authorities were conspiring against him and his rebellious talent. Joyce hinted at this conspiracy in a letter to Lady Gregory, but she instead urged him to continue his medical studies at Dublin's Trinity College. Her plea was bound to be unsuccessful: the young author envisioned the school "set heavily in the city's ignorance like a great dull stone set in a cumbrous ring," and he longed to evade his country's "national disease" of "provincialness, wind-and-piss philosophizing, crookedness, vacuity, and a verbal spouting that reserved sentiment for God and for the dead."

This harsh assessment indicates two further reasons Joyce felt compelled to leave his homeland. First, he was finding himself increasingly opposed to the Roman Catholic Church, the most powerful of institutions in Ireland, and his recent loss of faith placed him in uncomfortable conflict with his religiously devout mother. As much as he regretted this personal discord, Joyce was unapologetic in his apostasy; he considered the Church an opponent of ambitious youth such as himself, as his explanation to Lady Gregory makes clear: "I want to achieve myself—little or great as I may be—for I know that there is no heresy or no philosophy which is so abhorrent to my church as a human being, and accordingly I am going to Paris." Joyce adds that although he has been driven out of his country as a misbeliever, "I have found no man yet with a faith like mine." But this faith was of a personal sort: instead of Catholicism, the young Joyce had embraced a position of humanism, or more precisely, a humanism-of-one: himself.

This self-centeredness leads to the second reason for Joyce's compulsion. No matter that he was only twenty and had published practically nothing; Joyce frankly felt he and his literary ambitions had outgrown the narrow-minded Irish multitude and the backwards-looking literary tastes of the Gaelic Revival. Although the poet William Butler Yeats had been criticized by Joyce for writing folk plays for the Abbey Theatre, Yeats's encouragement still assumes the cosmopolitan values he was accused of abandoning. Responding to Joyce's lyrical poems and prose "epiphanies," Yeats writes, "The work which you have actually done is very remarkable for a man of your age *who has lived away from the vital intellectual centres.*" Joyce was determined to relocate to one of these "intellectual centres," and instead of being the latest of his literary countrymen—George Bernard Shaw, Oscar Wilde, and Yeats himself—to live in London, he would follow his own path, venturing boldly to Paris and enjoying there the "fair courts of life."

For several reasons, then, Joyce's departure from Dublin's Kingstown pier (which he suggestively called a "disappointed bridge") on the evening of December 1, 1902, achieved a symbolic resonance, as would similar farewells—realized or not—in his work. The climax of the story "Eveline" takes place at the North Wall, site of the piers, where the title character is set to explore a better life with Frank, her paramour who is about to sail to Buenos Aires. From the station Eveline glimpses "the black mass of the boat, lying in beside the quay wall, with illumined portholes." The boat's whistle is matched by a bell that clangs upon her heart—she will not, cannot follow him. Frank is a known figure for the author, and Joyce may have invested Eveline with a personification of Dublin itself: "Her eyes gave him no sign of love or farewell or recognition."

A more pertinent turning point occurs in *A Portrait of the Artist as a Young Man*, where the even more autobiographical hero Stephen Dedalus begins one of his final journal entries with "Away! Away!" He soon describes the "black arms of tall ships that stand against the moon, their tale of distant nations," a penetrating description of the masts and steamers lining the River Liffey, as seen from the North Wall. Stephen's mother helps him pack and prays for her son "that [he] may learn in [his] own life and away from home and friends what the heart is and what it feels. Amen. So be it." Joyce in the conclusion to *A Portrait* captures the energy, exuberance, and artistic ambition that surely buoyed him as he approached the North Sea through the "spectacle of Dublin's commerce":

Welcome, O Life! I go to encounter for the millionth time
the reality of experience and to forge in the smithy of my
soul the uncreated conscience of my race.

Sailing through the night, Joyce arrived early the next morning at London's Euston Station. He was met there by a sleepy Yeats, who at least found his traveling guest "unexpectedly amiable." Their visit was a culmination of sorts. Earlier that summer Joyce had made a concentrated effort to introduce himself to Dublin's most important literary figures. He began with George Russell, a poet and mystic who wrote under the pseudonym "AE." Their first meeting was a colorful one, with Joyce visiting a surprised Russell after midnight and, upon being asked to read his poetry, made it clear that he did not care in the least about his host's opinion. The young writer had obviously made an impression on Russell, as much for his promise as for his dismissive criticisms of fellow writers. "There is a young boy named Joyce who may do something," Russell writes to one friend. "He is proud as Lucifer," a fitting simile to describe a young man whose boyish amusements included playing Satan to his siblings' Adam and Eve!

He announced his "young genius" to the novelist George Moore, who recalled an essay of Joyce's as "preposterously clever," to Lady Gregory, and finally to Yeats: "The first spectre of the new generation has appeared," writes Russell, with a messianic rhetoric Joyce would soon unabashedly attribute for himself. Russell was not, however, without a certain bemusement: "I have suffered for him and I would like you to suffer." And so in early October Yeats agreed, visiting this "extremely clever boy" at a café near the National Library.

Although he later revealed an "immense admiration" for Yeats, Joyce cultivated an audacious self-confidence in preparing for this meeting. "I am not, as you see, treating you with any deference, for after all both you and I will be forgotten," Joyce explained to his artistic elder. When Yeats mentioned his reading of Balzac and Swinburne, the other burst out laughing at these old-fashioned tastes, drawing the attention of the entire café. In an unpublished preface Yeats recollects Joyce's boast of throwing over metrical form in his epiphanies "that he might get a form so fluent that it would respond to the motions of the spirit." At first he thought he had Joyce all figured out—he was the latest version of the critical Catholic firebrand from the Royal University. But then Joyce spoke with displeasure about Oscar Wilde's deathbed conversion, regretting that he had been "untrue to himself at the end." It seemed the young man was more complex than Yeats had presumed. As they concluded their meeting, Joyce said with a sigh, "I have met you too late. You are too old."

In *Autobiographies* Yeats would speak of a "young poet, who wrote excellently but had the worst manners," yet he would continue to show

Joyce a mentor's patient generosity. In early November he responded to news of Joyce's Paris trip and tutoring plans with a gentle sagacity, understated in its advice:

> I think you should let me give you one or two literary introductions here in London as you will find it much easier to get on in Paris (where perhaps a great many people do not want to learn English) if you do some writing, book reviews, poems etc.

On the morning of Joyce's arrival, Yeats offered him a sofa "to sleep off the fatigue of the journey," a few meals, and most importantly, appointments with editors at the *Academy* and *Speaker*, periodicals that offered freelance work. In the evening Yeats introduced him to Arthur Symons, an influential translator and critic of French literature who would assist Joyce in publishing some poems.

That night Joyce crossed the Channel to Dieppe and continued by train to Paris, where he took a room in the Latin Quarter at the Hotel Corneille. (The hotel was known for housing down-and-out British travelers.) Lady Gregory had expressed concern to Yeats that their "poor boy" would "knock his ribs against the earth," but she did what she could. She smartly prevented Joyce from seeing one friend, a "devout Catholic Churchman" (!), and managed to introduce him to the Irish playwright J.M. Synge, one Parisian pauper who could give "practical advice" to another. She also secured for him a reviewing job at the *Daily Express*, a Dublin paper.

Lady Gregory also arranged for Joyce to contact a physician in Paris, via a letter from a London acquaintance. This tenuous relationship might have discouraged others, but Joyce immediately sought out the doctor, and afterwards raved about the seven courses he had been fed when he first wrote his family. (His brother Stanislaus would remark in his diary that they were living "on practically starvation rations," making this sunny letter home an early example of Joyce's characteristic insensitivity to his family's plight.)

At first Joyce was full of updates and orders for his family. He had bought an alarm clock to avoid missing classes, which he began attending in early December. (He presently found the lectures too technical for his French.) His younger brother Stanislaus dutifully filled the roles of middleman and messenger, being asked in a single letter to pick up and forward some paper, to send a recent magazine, to write a publisher, and "to be careful of the books in my room." Often he would ask Stanislaus to send various quantities of these books, to request review books from editors, or to retrieve other books from pawn shops. By mid-month Joyce was complaining of illness, and he must have been much relieved when his parents decided he should return to Dublin for the holidays (a voyage for which his father took that second mortgage). His first "exile" was a trip of two weeks.

To celebrate his pending return, Joyce played the part of local gallant, the type he would later describe in *Ulysses*: "Faces of Paris men go by, their wellpleased pleasers, curled conquistadores." He visited a theater, a brothel, and a photo parlor, where he ordered three postcards with his portrait—vague expression, oversized black trenchcoat, and a hat that made him resemble either an Ulster minister or a toy monkey looking for cymbals to crash.

The first card was sent, with requisite money worries, to his family. To one friend (J. F. Byrne) he sent a new poem about the "journeyings of the soul," an altogether derivative lyric strongly influenced by the "Celtic Twilight," despite his criticism of the movement. Less exaltedly, he sent another friend (Vincent Cosgrave) a short "treatise" on French prostitutes, composed in dog-Latin. The trio of cards demonstrates his three competing sides—the bourgeois son, slightly overwhelmed; the pensive artist with his deep thoughts; and the college rogue quick to brag about his new moral freedoms.

Returning to Paris in the new year, Joyce pursued his journalistic opportunities in earnest, in part from financial necessity and partly to gain a desired literary credibility. He often expressed an annoyed ingratitude to his parents—he couldn't cash their money order because it arrived too late, or he was disappointed that their "connections" weren't more effective: "It is strange that I have been able to do more with strangers than you can do with friends," he wrote petulantly, although his mother kets insisting he pay a visit to Maude Gonne, the object of Yeats' melancholy affections, writing "YOU CANNOT GET ON IN YOUR LINE WITHOUT FRIENDS." Often his sarcasm about being unable to buy food bordered on manipulative cruelty: "Two meals in 60 hours is not bad, I think." At other times he blamed his ailments on fasting, and lamented being the only one starving in Paris during Carnival. He also berated his mother occasionally, writing "When you spend only three minutes at a letter it cannot be very intelligible."

For such correspondence the Irish novelist Edna O'Brien, Joyce's most recent biographer, accuses him of being "monstrously indifferent" to his mother's situation. Though not necessarily inaccurate, her censure of Joyce belies the complexity of his situation. His self-absorption is slightly more permissible when his family's own feelings are considered. They were highly conscious of Joyce's French residence as a strategic gambit, a literary pad from which their son with his "great thoughts" could launch himself. His ambition was a point of family pride, so naturally John Joyce wrote to his son like an Irish Lord Chesterfield, presiding over the Dublin slums: should Joyce hold his grandfather's noble ideas he would be sure to "not do anything unbecoming a gentleman."

By March, with Joyce's confidence growing, his family had several reasons to be proud. His reviews were appearing in print, and he was spending days amid the busy austerity of the Bibliothèque Nationale and evenings in the Bibliothèque Sainte-Geneviève, reading Aristotle and Aquinas and keeping an aesthetics notebook, which would serve him well when writing his first novel *Stephen Hero* and its later incarnation, *A Portrait of the Artist as a Young Man*. Joyce's mother continued to take care of her son steadfastly; in her letters she forbade him to drink Paris's water unless he boiled it and urged him to be *very careful* with the little stove he hoped to buy. Her offer to clean his soiled suit and pay for the postage to do so, thus saving him a few shillings at the laundry, exemplified the maternal kindness of which self-centered youth so often and so effortlessly take advantage.

Finally, Joyce was unaware of the one fact that in retrospect makes his selfishness so damnable. In early April a blunt telegram from his father informed him: "Mother dying come home Father." Joyce's single, emotional sentence home—"Dear Mother Please write to me at once if you can and tell me what is wrong"—reflects the child he still was, despite having come of age two months earlier. His terse response to his father's telegram foreshadows the detachment he would shortly assume: "Arrive morning Jim."

"I WILL NOT SERVE."

Joyce returned to Dublin on Easter Sunday 1903, an ironic landing in light of the inevitable quarrel looming—a showdown between a good Catholic mother, now dying, and her now faithless son, unwilling to go through the prayerful motions, or to show even a modicum of piety. The painful conflict was imminent; Joyce's earliest days, in contrast had passed happily enough.

James Joyce was born on February 2, 1882, in Rathgar, a well-to-do suburb of south Dublin. Aside from an earlier child who had died at birth, he was the eldest son of John and May Joyce. His father's family claimed descent from Norman-Irish stock in Galway, and Joyce's grandfather improved their fortunes by marrying into the prosperous O'Connells of County Cork. His grandmother later took their twenty-something son to Dublin to better direct his desultory energy. He impressed new friends with his fine tenor voice and, after a brief and aborted attempt at running a brewery, took up politics thanks to a bit of nepotism—a relative was Lord Mayor at the time. Consequently he enjoyed a well-paid, easy-going job (it was practically a sinecure) under the Collector of Rates.

This tax collector soon met his bride in a local church choir: May Murray, ten years his junior and daughter of a wine agent. John Joyce disdained his wife's family as less worthy, and he passed these feelings to his son, who throughout his life would honor the suspect coat of arms of the Joyce clan. The family moved to Bray, a pleasant sea village, when Joyce was two. (John Joyce joked that the train fare would keep his wife's family in the city.) During that year Joyce's brother Stanislaus was born, his closest sibling.

"Once upon a time and a very good time it was" begin the recollections of *A Portrait of the Artist as a Young Man*. During this "good time" a great uncle from Cork moved in, and occasionally a nationalist radical visited secretly, trying to escape arrest. These merry, exciting times suited Joyce, who danced before his family. He was dubbed "Sunny Jim," while the more solemn Stanislaus became "Brother John." Also present was "Dante" Hearn Conway, the boys' first governess whose strong nationalism was only overridden by her stronger religiosity. In her instruction she exposed them to an apocalyptic piety, and warned the boys that they would go to hell for playing with a Protestant neighbor girl.

In 1888 the Joyces took their son twenty miles west of Dublin to Clongowes Wood College, whose manicured lawn and large turrets must have intimidated the boy. Clongowes was the best prepatory school in Ireland, and Joyce was its youngest student: when asked his age, he politely said, "half-past-six," which in turn became another nickname. The school was run by Jesuits, famous for their educational rigor, and the training Joyce received left its indelible mark, for good or bad. In *Ulysses* Buck Mulligan offers Stephen Dedalus a mock diagnosis, "You have the cursed jesuit strain in you, only it's injected the wrong way." Joyce later said of his education: "I have learnt to arrange things in such a way that they become easy to survey and to judge," a valuable skill for a modernist novelist. The attention to rhetoric and languages provided the foundation upon which he would develop his initially ornate style, his innovative "mimetic" narrative techniques, and his unmatched gifts for encyclopedic literary parody. (The last of these skills culminates masterfully in the "Circe" chapter of *Ulysses*, comprising with its progressive styles a veritable chronicle of the English language.)

Joyce was both happy and homesick during his three years at Clongowes. The older boys tormented him initially, often attacking the Joyces' inferior social standing. Another boy broke his glasses once, but the prefect—suspecting Joyce had broken them intentionally to avoid study—paddled *his* hands instead. Feeling victimized, he went straight to the rector in protest, an act that earned him some respect among his older classmates. (The incident becomes a scene in the first chapter of *A Portrait*.) On another occasion he fell sick with the "collywobbles" after being shoved into the cesspool near the boys' lavatory. Yet in spite of his young age he was surprisingly athletic, enjoying cricket and winning prize cups in hurdling and walking. He was also named an altar boy and wrote a hymn to the Virgin Mary, distinctions that of course pleased his mother.

The Joyce fortunes worsened with those of their political hero Charles Parnell, Ireland's "uncrowned king." Parnell's adultery with Kitty O'Shea was made public in November 1890, and after he was abandoned by Tim Healy and other allies, his party was divided a month later. The events precipitated Parnell's death the following October, and the 9-year-old Joyce responded by writing an angry poem, "Et Tu, Healy," comparing Parnell's disloyal comrade with Brutus, Julius Caesar's conspirator. His proud father had it printed and distributed among his friends.

John Joyce had already withdrawn his son from Clongowes because of finances, and his stout defense of the "Chief" Parnell was held against him: He lost his tax-collector position, had to sell family properties to complement under-collected amounts, and only received a modest pension through the intervention of his wife. He would never again have regular employment, a casualty of his and Parnell's "enemies" at the age of 42. Joyce would hold his father's grudges, and Malcolm Brown in *The Politics of Irish Literature* suggests the author henceforth froze Irish politics "at the instant of the Parnellite disaster." In a lecture in Italy Joyce later summarized the tragedy: his countrymen had not thrown Parnell to the wolves, "they tore him to pieces themselves."

The Joyces moved to Blackrock early in 1892, and a year later yet again to Dublin proper. This residence off Mountjoy Square was their last "good" address. In Blackrock Joyce was permitted to study independently: he wrote poetry, began a novel, and constantly begged his mother to quiz him on facts and vocabulary. In the city he briefly attended the Christian Brothers' school, which must have been an educational shock: the brothers were soon called "Paddy Stinky and Mickey Mudd" by Joyce's father, whose chance meeting with the former rector of Clongowes brought Joyce's current schooling to a fortunate end. This rector now worked at nearby Belvedere College, a Jesuit day school, and he magnanimously arranged for Joyce and his brothers to attend tuition-free.

The following year Joyce and his father together returned to Cork, where John was forced to dissolve the last of his inherited properties. The income, however, provided no relief but instead went to a solicitor, unusually successful in recovering his loan. The family moved yet again, this time to Drumcondra, a working-class section of northern Dublin. Since Joyce's enrollment in Clongowes, seven more siblings had arrived, the latest being born the previous winter. John paired children with mortgages, and their latest residence was untimely in its smallness and comparatively non-descript.

For both boys it was a tumultuous time. Stanislaus fought with "Pisser" Duffy, a neighbor kid, and Joyce too endured a brawl. It began at school, when his writing instructor accused him of heresy in one of his assignments. Spurred by this encounter, a group of classmates followed Joyce home, arguing with him about the best poet. The boys obediently said Tennyson, but Joyce declared Byron, despite his bad reputation.

Beaten with a stick, his clothes torn, Joyce nevertheless had a new awareness of himself, a new sense of a noble solitude, having suffered for artistic truth both in mind and body.

The instructor's rebuke, however, was the exception to the rule: Joyce was at the height of his studiousness, winning scholastic prizes for three successive years. When spring examinations rolled around, the family treated him like royalty, knowing a significant monetary award was at stake. The Joyces had returned to Mountjoy Square late in 1894 and would stay there four years, their longest stint since the early years at Bray. As a student he must have benefited from a new (relative) stability, and he responded to his good academic fortune with generous gestures toward his family—taking them to dinner or the theatre, providing quick loans. In 1897 he won an additional prize for having written the best English composition from his grade in Ireland, yet by then he was already living a double life.

Now 14, Joyce was an adolescent dramatically discovering his sexuality. One night, walking home from the theatre, he encountered a prostitute on a path near the Royal Canal and "summoned the recklessness to indulge his curiosity." Though elected head of the Sodality of the Blessed Virgin (of which his mother was a life-long member) in the fall of 1896, he titillated himself by praying with lips still fresh from "a lewd kiss." His rector sensed something was afoot, and intimidated Stanislaus into confessing that his brother had dallied with the Joyces' maidservant. "Your son is inclined to evil ways," he warned Joyce's concerned mother.

Joyce recoiled from these ways briefly in the winter of 1896, after attending a retreat where he heard a sermon, vivid in the manner of St. Ignatius. (He dramatizes this event in *A Portrait's* middle chapter.) Immediately after the retreat he visited a chapel, where he made his first confession since Easter. A fervent spirituality reawakened, which he would describe thus: "He ran through his measure like a spendthrift saint, astonishing many by ejaculatory fervors, offending many by airs of the cloister." A sister saw him devotedly saying his rosary on the way to school, but this state of mind would not last. "I have amended my life, have I not?" Stephen asks in *A Portrait*. Joyce hadn't. The temptations of the flesh were too great, and like his hero he returned to his earlier burning: "He wanted to sin with another of his kind, to force another being to sin with him, and to exult with her in sin."

The enthusiasm of his spiritual reformation was followed by an equally powerful rejection, and as his Catholicism waned, his artistic commitments grew. He was writing a series of prose sketches entitled *Silhouettes* as well as *Moods*, a first poetry collection (both unfortunately lost). Visits to "Nighttown" continued less shamefully now, and he was a familiar enough customer that one prostitute encouraged him to enter a singing contest, offering to lend him the entry fee! He was also under watch at the local library for his "questionable" reading habits, requesting novels by George Meredith and Thomas Hardy. In his place he sometimes sent Stanislaus, who on a mission to acquire Hardy's *Jude the Obscure*, endeared himself to his brother by mistakenly asking for *Jude the Obscene*.

Concurrently Joyce treated women in a much different fashion, sublimating them into aesthetic objects of adoration. One such young woman was Mary Sheehy, whose family's house Joyce often visited for pleasant Sunday evenings of charades and song. Sheehy's father was a parliamentarian, and their more genteel setting contrasted strikingly with Joyce's clandestine rendezvouses with prostitutes.

In the summer of 1898, he saw a girl on the shore lifting her skirts above her ankles to avoid the tide. His imagination transformed her into a "strange and beautiful seabird." Joyce in developing his aesthetic theories called such an image an "epiphany." Eventually situating them within his fictional narratives, he first collected them separately in notebooks, as crystalline prose poems. Used by the Church to describe the wise men's visit to the infant Jesus, "epiphany" nicely symbolizes the deflection of Joyce's religious devotion toward his devoted artistry. A conversation he had with Stanislaus further reveals the religious overtones of his technique:

> Don't you think there is a certain resemblance between the mystery of the Mass and what I am trying ... to give people some kind of intellectual pleasure or spiritual enjoyment by converting the bread of everyday life into something that has a more permanent artistic life of its own.... It is my idea of the significance of trivial things that I want to give the two or three unfortunate wretches who may eventually read me.

The critic Harry Levin concisely summarizes an epiphany as "the single word that tells the whole story ... the simple gesture that reveals a complex set of relationships." In *A Portrait* Stephen speaks of "the *whatness* of a thing," and this feminine beach vision fills him with "profane joy." Just before seeing her, Stephen's "soul had arisen from the grave of boyhood," and the young woman seemed to be the angel lifting him: "To live, to err, to fall, to triumph, to recreate life out of life! A wild angel had appeared to him, an angel of mortal youth and beauty," a sacred Muse, as Beatrice was to Joyce's exile-hero, Dante.

The angel image helpfully suggests the most important literary influence on Joyce at this time: the Norwegian playwright Henrik Ibsen, the aloof arbiter of an equally provincial people. ("To live is to war with the trolls," he had written.) In his capacity to create an idealized irony in his plays, sometimes savage—the Dublin papers thought him "coarse" or "immoral"—and always honest, Ibsen is said in *Stephen Hero* to have the temper of an archangel. His example would supply Joyce with a ruthlessness (which Stanislaus thought the keynote of his brother's work) while still uplifting him, calling him forth to the precipice of artistic purity.

Joyce would henceforth hold the drama in new esteem, viewing it in *A Portrait* as the genre where the artist "like the God of the creation remains within or behind or beyond or above his handiwork, invisible, refined out of existence, indifferent, paring his fingernails." Thus he attended the theatre regularly, and after a particular performance made one of his characteristic prophecies. He and his family the night before had seen a play whose subject was "genius breaking out in the home and against the home." Their assured son flatly said, "You nedn't have gone to see it. It's going to happen in your own house."

Renewed with an artist's vision, Joyce, 16, entered University College in the fall. John Henry Cardinal Newman in 1853 had founded it as the Catholic University, occupying part of Stephen's Green in crumbling magnificence. It was incorporated into the more secular Royal University system in the 1870s before the Jesuits took it over a decade later, with the poet Gerard Manley Hopkins holding the chair in classics. Joyce got along well with his Italian lecturer, Father Charles Ghezzi, with whom he further discussed Dante and Gabriele D'Annunzio, a contemporary novelist they both respected. Joyce's readings in Church history signaled his rebellious position, including fiery clerics such as Joachim di Fiore and Giordano Bruno, the latter a victim of the Roman Inquisition in 1600. Once Ghezzi reminded Joyce that Bruno was a "terrible heretic," and his pupil coolly responded, "Yes, and he was terribly burned."

The young man's demeanor, as the preceding reply may indicate, had changed. He approached his studies nonchalantly, instead wandering around the city with wrinkled clothes and body unwashed. (He apparently took a strange pride in the lice that accosted him!) In the spring of 1899 Joyce had the opportunity to act upon his individualist postures. Yeats's play *The Countless Cathleen* premiered to much controversy, being perceived as anti-Ireland and anti-Church. Joyce attended with his friends, all of whom joined in the booing and hissing that met the play. They objected to the Irish being represented as "a loathsome brood of appostates," and signed a patriotic protest letter that appeared in the *Freeman's Journal*. Joyce was the only member of his class who refused to sign.

The next school year Joyce worked carefully on an essay, "Drama and Life," which he arranged to deliver before the college Literary and Historical Society. Initially forbidden to read it, Joyce persevered, finally doing so on January 20, 1900. Greek and Shakespearean dramas were dead, he declared with youthful gusto, and he advocated a realism that would influence the short stories he was soon to compose. "Life we must accept as we see it before our eyes, men and women as we meet them in the real world, not as we apprehend them in the world of faery." Unsurprisingly he praised the work of Ibsen as being "of universal import," and he continued brooding on his literary master in the article "Ibsen's New Drama," which the prestigious London periodical *Fortnightly Review* published in April. The accomplishment stunned his classmates, as the twelve guineas he received fueled their envy.

Good news, to be sure, but Joyce could not have anticipated the annunciation he soon received. At the end of April he received a letter from William Archer, the English translator of Ibsen who was passing on the great thanks of the Norwegian playwright himself. (From what he could gather of the English review, Ibsen had found Joyce's words "very benevolent.") Joyce sent his appreciation, identifying himself as "a young Irishman, eighteen years old." In May he invited his father to London, financing their travels with the income from Joyce's article. They spent much of their time at theatres and music halls, though Joyce also paid several visits to various editors, in search of journalistic work. (The *Fortnightly* editor was surprised to find his recent contributor so young.) When they returned to Dublin, Joyce grandly pronounced to Stanislaus, "The music hall, not poetry, is a criticism of life."

Yet Joyce was never fully to be a "people's poet." He spent the next two summers in Mullingar, a rural market town in central Ireland, where his father had been hired to organize the voting lists. Urban middle-class in his upbringing and surroundings, Joyce would never romanticize the peasantry as Yeats and others did. He instead seemed intent on scandalizing them, saying things such as, "My mind is more interesting to me than the entire country," which I suppose is an apt statement, however obnoxious, for one who wished to be a "priest of the eternal imagination." The first summer there he wrote a play, *A Brilliant Career*, the "first true work of my life," which he pompously dedicated to "my own soul."

He was also working on a verse drama, *Dream Stuff*, and a poem cycle, *Shine and Dark*, both of whose titles make us somewhat less regretful that the works themselves haven't survived. Afterward Joyce sent the play and some poems to William Archer, who replied to the submissions by saying he was both a great deal impressed and bewildered; he would be an important source of encouragement for the next two years.

Joyce sent a letter to Ibsen in honor of the playwright's 73rd birthday in March 1901. He wrote it in Dano-Norwegian (remarkably), but an earlier English version exists: "I have sounded your name defiantly through the college where it was either unknown or known faintly and darkly." He says Ibsen's battles and inward heroism have inspired him, and yet he concludes his respects in a strangely eulogistic tone: "Your work on earth draws to a close and you are near your silence. It is growing dark for you.... You have opened the way ... But I am sure that higher and holier enlightenment lies—onward." With typical audacity, Joyce frames Ibsen as a literary "Henrik the Baptist" whose work has proclaimed the advent of a new kingdom, of a greater, Irish messiah.

Again in Mullingar that summer, Joyce translated two plays by the German writer Gerhard Hauptmann, and he hoped the Irish Literary Theatre would produce them. It declined in the fall, which caused Joyce in his indignance to write an essay denouncing the theatre and the provincial nature of its revival. "The Day of the Rabblement" begins with a sabre-rattling statement allusively attributed to Giordano Bruno: "No man, said the Nolan, can be a lover of the true or the good unless he abhors the multitude," which is followed by attacks on most of the Irish literary figures of the day.

The magazine *St. Stephen's* refused to print the essay, which led Joyce to publish it privately. Its author at this point was not really hated by his classmates, but he also wasn't taken altogether seriously, generally being thought of as "raving mad" or as "dreamy Jimmy." (He was allowed to speak again before the Literary & Historical Society the following spring, 1902, but this time in defense of an overlooked Irish poet.)

In his essay Joyce claims that the best Irish artists were mere "giantlings," and none had emerged yet "of European stature." Ibsen is, naturally, given pride of place, with Hauptmann hailed as his successor. In a now familiar rhetorical move, Joyce as a self-aggrandizing prophet speaks of a "third minister" who "will not be wanting when his hour comes. Even now that hour may be standing by the door." Richard Ellman, Joyce's most authoritative biographer, correctly pinpoints Ibsen's acknowledgement of his follower as the beginning of Joyce's turning toward the Continent: "Before Ibsen's letter Joyce was an Irishman; after it he was European."

And so went his literary tastes, Stanislaus recording in his diary how his brother often boasted "of being modern." A writer for *St. Stephen's*, probably put off by Joyce's strong opinions, responded tongue-in-cheek to the controversy. Pretending to quote from state papers belonging to Queen Elizabeth, he says Joyce, who has been "corrupted, as we do verily believe, by the learning of Italie or othere foreigne parts, hath no care for Holye Religion." The anonymous scribe was prophetic in his own right, and those "othere forreigne parts" would become a physical reality in that first trip to Paris later in the year.

"How I hate God and death! How I like Nora!"

When Joyce found his confidence in Paris in the spring of 1903, he imagined his literary career as already mapped out: a book of songs to be published in 1907, a comedy five years later, his "Esthetic" in another five years. ("This *must* interest you," he wrote his mother, one hopes, sarcastically.) In the same letter he proudly informs her of a classmate's impressed judgment of his move to Paris: "There is something sublime in Joyce's standing alone."

Returning to his confrontation with his dying mother, it is best to remember he had been standing alone for some time. Joyce's rejection of his Catholic faith resulted in an essential distance between them. He became aware, as he says in *A Portrait*, "of a first noiseless sundering of their lives." The painful events which followed after his return to Dublin were likely inevitable. In any case they were definitive and would remain in the author's psyche for many years.

Ellman astutely describes Joyce's return as "filial but anticlimatic." May Joyce's situation had improved slightly thus her death would come more slowly. Suffering from liver cancer, she often vomited green bile into a basin. On her better days she was anxious that Joyce, whom she called "the mocker," go to confession and take communion. He refused his Easter duties, and the mother wept for her apostate son.

He sought sympathy from his friend Byrne and his Aunt Josephine, but both felt his stubborn refusals were unnatural and cruel. A mother's love is the one sure thing in the world, says Cranly, Byrne's character in *A Portrait*. "Your mother brings you into the world, carries you first in her body." Delivering a child is suffering enough, he argues, and Stephen should not make his mother suffer more by his intellectual convictions. "Every jackass going the roads thinks he has ideas," Cranly says victoriously.

But Stephen counters. His confirmation name (like his author's) is Aloysius, a saint who rejected his mother's embrace for the sake of higher callings. Elsewhere Stephen strives to replace both his religion and his "debt" to his mother, indeed the woman herself: "In the virgin womb of the imagination the word was made flesh." Joyce had dutifully reported his attendance at religious service in Paris, but his true motives were finally different: His Easter Week experience in Notre-Dame may have comforted his mother, but it more permanently found its place in *Finnegans Wake* years later.

Unpardoned, Joyce turned to different, less principled friends. One was Oliver St. John Gogarty, a wealthier companion, more of a dandy, and currently returned from his studies at Oxford. He lent Joyce nicer clothes and soon accompanied him on all-night drinking bouts. "I should be supported at the expense of the state because I am capable of enjoying life," Joyce boasted to Stanislaus, who recorded his brother coming home drunk three or four times a week, a pace matched by their father and younger brother, Charles. Joyce tended to make other writers endure his surly, despondent moods, and he soon found himself uninvited to literary events hosted by Lady Gregory and George Moore.

At home May was worsening, and during the last week of her life Joyce sang her Yeats's "Who Goes with Fergus?" a lyric he had also sung to his dying brother George two years before. John Joyce was by this time exhausted and volatile in his grief. One night he screamed at his wife, "If you can't get well, die. Die and be damned to you!" Stanislaus attacked him, and Joyce succeeded in locking his father in a separate room. She died on August 13, 1903, and although the boys' uncle ordered them to kneel before her in prayer, both refused. In the aftermath Joyce read through his parents' love letters, coldly looking for material. "Nothing," he informed Stanislaus before they burnt them. John Joyce was devastated and became tyrannical and abusive, drinking even more heavily.

The Joyce family had moved several more times since Joyce entered and graduated from college. When he had received his word of Ibsen's gratitude, they were living in Fairview, adjacent to a convent from which they heard the screams of mad nuns. This image finds its way into *A Portrait*, and it effectively suggests the pity Joyce ultimately felt toward his mother, viewing her as a faithful, but sacrificial, servant, as much for her country as her family. His feelings for her were probably caught up in his more complicated view of women in general. He had recently spoken of women as "soft-skinned animals" to Stanislaus, odd in itself and further complicated by the symbolic roles women would play in his work. There the Church is portrayed as "the scullerymaid of christendom," and Irish womanhood "a batlike soul waking to the consciousness of itself in darkness and secrecy and loneliness."

Whatever his views, Joyce would be haunted by his mother's death and his handling of it. "Agenbite of inwit," or remorse of conscience, is a leitmotif throughout *Ulysses*, which opens with Stephen pondering his loss and guilt: "Silently, in a dream she had come to him after her death, her wasted body within its loose brown grave-clothes ..." Buck Mulligan accuses him of killing his mother "by telling her what he thought," to which Stephen defensively replies, "Cancer did it not I." Later in the phantasmagoric "Circe" episode, his mother appears as a character saying, "I pray for you in my other world.... Years and years I loved you, O my son, my firstborn, when you lay in my womb." Finally, in his play *Exiles*, which would not be written for a decade, Joyce anachronistically uses his future family to explain a rift between a mother and son; interestingly the mother in the play refuses reconcilement, and the protagonist is justified in a way Joyce feared he hadn't been:

RICHARD: While she lived she turned aside from me and from mine. That is certain.
BEATRICE: From you and from ... ?
RICHARD: From Bertha and from me and from our child. And so I waited for the end, as you say. And it came.

Joyce recovered somewhat in the fall after his mother's death and began writing again, publishing 19 reviews before being fired from the Dublin *Daily Express*, which he welcomed. He tended to wear black, like Hamlet. Joyce sought a position at the National Library and was turned down; he was asked to teach some evening French classes at his alma mater, but he refused, fearing in his paranoia an attempt to make him dependent. He even attended a few law classes, at his father's urging. In the winter Joyce approached an old classmate about starting a halfpenny daily newspaper called *The Goblin*. Their ideal benefactor declined to fund the operation, despite, or perhaps because of, his generous support of the more earnest and trustworthy Padraic Colum. Joyce was disgusted.

In his dissatisfaction he flirted for a while with socialism and anarchism, but he was never a very serious member of anything. His reading of Nietzsche did provide a philosophical support of his sneers and jeers toward all things conventional, and in the following year he would sign himself "James Overman," a playful allusion to the Nietzschean "Ubermensch." He had given up on gainful employment by 1904, a concession that proved most important. Stanislaus's decision to quit his clerkship and join his brother in "sensitive inactivity" (Ellman's wonderful phrase) was equally important, for he was Joyce's most important audience, the whetstone—they both admitted it— against which the elder could sharpen the knife of his growing artistry.

On January 7 Joyce wrote in one sitting "A Portrait of the Artist as a Young Man," a modest essay that would have major ramifications for his later fiction. He opens by defending his new fictional methods, speaking of a "fluid succession of presents," an "individuating rhythm," and a "curve of an emotion." He would later complain that English novelists "always keep beating about the bush;" one might say he was about to put ice skates on the feet of modern fiction, letting the language shift unconsciously and implicitly suggest, subtly reflecting a character's changing settings.

He had composed the essay for *Dana*, a new literary journal that promptly rejected the submission. He decided it wasn't complete and began what would become *Stephen Hero*, his autobiographical novel, "as he usually [began] things, half in anger, to show that in writing about himself he has a subject of more interest than their aimless discussion" (Stanislaus's impression). Yet Joyce was also learning not to take his subject so seriously, recognizing the unpleasant or merely laughable aspects of his doppelganger hero. He memorably comments on his own verbosity in *A Portrait* by interrupting Stephen's starchy speech on "The Greek, the Turk, the Chinese, the Copt" with an approaching cart's "harsh roar of jangled and rattling metal."

He was, however, still prone to overwriting, reflected in Stanislaus's acute criticism that Joyce "is thought to be very frank about himself but his style is such that it might be contended that he confesses in a foreign language"—in other words, in florid language more appropriate for the delicate lyrics that would become *Chamber Music*, which he was also writing at this time. Gogarty offers a humorous if not entirely accurate version of how his friend's poetry collection received its name. One night they visited a less than mournful widow, whom Joyce entertained by reading his poems. She liked them well enough, but had to excuse herself to use a chamberpot behind a screen. "There's a critic for you!" Gogarty howled. Later Stanislaus, solemn as ever, said the incident should be considered a "favorable omen" of his choice of title.

Joyce finished the first chapter of his novel in early February, and very quickly certain friends became irritated at the thought of being characters in Joyce's fiction. Gogarty complained they were "accessories before the fact." He had never been a completely trustworthy friend to Joyce, telling someone once that he would make his friend drink "to break his spirit," and their relationship would soon worsen. Byrne, who Joyce felt had betrayed him, became known as "His Particular Intensity" in the latter's correspondence. To be fair, these friends were not completely unmerited in their feelings; later Joyce would give Stanislaus a threatening message for his friend Vincent Cosgrave: "Tell him also that I am going to write a 'Dubliner' on him," as if his short stories were written fisticuffs to distribute among his friends.

Joyce continued writing through the spring of 1904 and resumed his fitful pursuit of his singing career. He impressed the city's best voice coach, but his lessons were intermittent, dependent on his cash flow. Competing in the Festival of Music, he would have won the gold medal had he not refused to read music at sight, which he felt was beneath a truly artistic singer. When Gogarty invited him to make a visit to Oxford, Joyce concocted a slightly more merry singing gig—a minstrel's lute tour through England's southern coast towns "like the Emperor Nero's tour in Greece." Joyce also held a few-week's tenure as a schoolteacher in Dalkey, a southern suburb. This briefest of careers would shape an early episode of *Ulysses*, but not much more. The young schoolmaster remained restless, as he couldn't yet know that his life was about to change forever.

Walking down Nassau Street on June 10, Joyce saw a tall young woman with auburn hair and a proud stride. He was instantly enamored by her and introduced himself. She mistook him for a sailor, with his yachting cap and canvas shoes. Her lilting accent clued him immediately to what he soon learned: she was a country-girl from Galway, recently arrived in Dublin and working as a chambermaid in Finn's Hotel. Their first date was a walk around Ringsend on June 16, 1904, a date later immortalized as "Bloomsday," the day on which the entire action of *Ulysses* occurs. In a scheme meant to explain the novel's complexity, Joyce called it, among other things, "a little story of a day (life)." His setting this "life" on the day of his first date with Nora is his most lasting, touching tribute to her, though so often in their subsequent life she would quite understandably have preferred more material tributes, such as groceries, or coal for the fire, or money for the landlady. But the hard days remained in the future.

Nora Barnacle, the daughter of a baker, lived with her grand-parents after her parents separated. A friend's memories of she and Nora stealing penny candies and dressing up as men to "ramble round the square" suggest the earthy, vivacious woman with whom Joyce quickly fell in love. She had only a grammar school education, and fled Galway to escape an abusive uncle. When Joyce's father first heard her somewhat comical last name, he declared with a straight face, "She'll never leave him."

Within a month Joyce was writing "Little Pouting Nora" or "My dear little Goodie-Brown-Shoes," and reporting that her glove lay beside him all night. The poet Ezra Pound would later say the "real" Joyce was the author of the lyrical poems, "the sensitive," and he now wasted none of these instincts in nobly praising his beloved: "I will tell you this that your soul seems to me to be the most beautiful and simple soul in the world," and:

> Why should I not call you what in my heart I continually call you? What is it that prevents me unless it be that no word is tender enough to be your name?
>
> JIM

Yet this paramour was not always of the high-minded, chivalrous sort. A racy sensuality frequently runs through their early correspondence, and sometimes our troubadour is downright randy, as when he sacrilegiously plays a cardinal, invested with apostolic powers by the pope, telling Nora to "come without skirts to receive the Papal Benediction which I shall be pleased to give you." Papal Rome had never sounded so decadent! He found in Nora someone who could absorb his complex and contradictory demands, who could be both faithful and tender as well as coarse and dominating. She could be his angel and taskmaster, as when he speaks of their intimacies from their first date as "a sacrament which left in me a final sense of sorrow and degradation." She would never be his betrayer, although he sometimes thought—and wished—her to be so.

Nora's letters, as Joyce would be the first to admit, were more capable of capturing simultaneously both the high-minded and passionate tones of lovers. Her first letter to him, on flowery stationery, is an intricate Victorian mess soon discovered to be copied from a letterbook. Joyce for good reason encouraged her to write in her own voice, as henceforth she breathlessly does:

> it was two o Clock when I got to bed I sat all the time like a fool thinking of you I longed for the time to come when I would not have to leave you ... Dear Jim I feel so lonely to night I dont know what to say it is useless for me to sit down and write when I would prefer to be with you I hope you will

have good news when I see you tomorrow night I will try to get out 8-15 Giving you all my thoughts till then

NORA

Her prose, as well as that of Joyce's mother, contributed to the free-flowing, unpunctuated brilliance of *Ulysses'* "Penelope" episode, comprising Molly Bloom's carnal yet lyrical recollections as she falls asleep: "and first I put my arms around him yes and drew him down so he could feel my breasts all perfume yes and his heart was going like mad and yes I said yes I will yes."

Joyce certainly didn't change other aspects of his life for Nora's sake. He continued to drink heavily and was beaten up after he approached a girl in Stephen's Green without first noticing her boyfriend. (That evening one significant thing did occur: he was kindly escorted home by Alfred H. Hunter, a Jew whose wife was cheating on him. This Good Samaritan proved to be a model for Leopold Bloom, the protagonist of *Ulysses*.) When he was sober Joyce was passing chapters of *Stephen Hero* among his friends and shamelessly borrowing money wherever he thought prospects existed. George Russell, looking to throw some work Joyce's way, asked if he could write some short stories—something simple, rural—that wouldn't shock readers of the *Irish Homestead*.

What resulted from this favor was a trio of stories—"The Sisters," "Eveline," and "After the Race"—which would eventually appear in the collection *Dubliners*. Joyce approached these stories with a "scrupulous meanness," his goal being "to betray the soul of that hemiplegia or paralysis which many consider a city." He more evocatively explains his judgment to Nora in a letter around the same time: "There is no life here—no naturalness or honesty. People live together in the same houses all their lives and at the end they are as far apart as ever."

Rejecting the romanticism or redemptive stoicism of Yeats and others, Joyce composed his new work with a naturalism nevertheless enriched by the symbolic power of his epiphanies. Furthermore, his "interior" style was developing, and by sentence rhythms and images he was increasingly able to reflect the numbed, wounded minds of his characters. He received a pound apiece for the stories, and "The Sisters" was published on the first anniversary of his mother's death. Though grateful for the income, he was ashamed to have his name appear in "the pigs' paper." So he signed himself "Stephen Dedalus." He submitted other stories, but the editor rejected them, having received many complaints about the earlier work.

By the end of the summer Joyce was "coming clean" to Nora, wondering if she could love him if she knew him fully. He seemed already to be considering a life abroad with her, having shared one of his more intoxicating epiphanies from his Paris days. "While I was repeating this to myself I knew that that life was still waiting for me if I chose to enter it," he writes. Confessing his spendthrift habits, the "open war" he makes upon the Catholic Church, the sordid course of his sexual experiences, he tested her love as the young Malcolm tests MacDuff's loyalty in *Macbeth*. Yet he ultimately wanted to stand before her and have his heart accepted: "Can you not see the simplicity which is at the back of all my disguises?"

Joyce had not lived with his family, now residing in Cabra, since a month after his mother's death, and with increasing frequency he found lodgings only by the good will of friends, unsuspecting acquaintances, and his aunt Josephine. In early September he moved in with Gogarty, who was renting the Martello Tower at Sandycove. Stark and thick-walled, the tower had been built a century earlier to defend against Napoleonic invasion. Next door there was and is a "gentleman's bath," but visitors should enter at their own risk: the water is cold enough to break your ankles, and the changing shed is for members of the Forty Foot Club only. Once they saw Yeats's father walking below on the beach, and Joyce asked him for two shillings. The elder Yeats said he had no money, and suspected drink was involved anyway.

These were the last of Joyce and Gogarty's friendly days. Stanislaus had heard Gogarty wished to kick Joyce out, but feared his guest would inflict authorial revenge. (He hardly had time to fear this before it came true, as Joyce had already written a satirical poem in which Gogarty and several others were roasted.) A second guest at the tower, a friend of Gogarty's from Oxford, hastened Joyce's departure in harrowing fashion. One night he started from a nightmare and crazily grabbed a revolver and discharged it, firing into the fireplace near where Joyce was sleeping. Joyce left immediately and the next day sent his fellow poet James Starkey to retrieve his trunk.

Flushed from his recent writing success, Joyce attempted to turn himself into a walking corporation, offering "shares" of himself and saying his stock would escalate as his work was published. (His peers of course thought him insane, but from the perspective of our own age, Joyce—for once—comes across as the prescient businessman.) More practically, he was already seeking teaching positions at various Berlitz schools on the Continent. He was encouraged in his quest by Byrne (with whom he had reconciled) and received his father's blessing, though he did so without mentioning Nora.

"Is there one who understands me?" Joyce cryptically asked his beloved, perhaps mimicking Hamlet's wrenching search for a confidant in Ophelia. "Yes," Nora replied, inferring from his question a veiled proposal. Her willingness to join him alternately frightened and exhilarated him. He asked if her family was wealthy, quickly explaining that he feared she would be deprived of accustomed comforts once abroad. "I often wonder do you realise thoroughly what you are about to do," he admonished her, and was gratified by her resolve: "The fact that you can choose to stand beside me in this way in my hazardous life feels me with great pride and joy."

Joyce received leads on teaching jobs in London and Amsterdam, but the couple was hoping for a position in Paris, "last of the human cities." Joyce was struck by the "amusing" quality of their pending adventures, and liked to imagine what his friends would think of he and Nora living together in the Latin Quarter. He began to seek a final round of handouts with extra vigor, dressing up one request by illogically telling an editor, "That is not exorbitant, as it is my last." Yeats' reply was particularly cold, and Lady Gregory wanted a more concrete plan. "Now I will make my own legend and stick to it," he replied in a huff. She relented, telegraphing him five pounds.

As he was passing around his "hat," he was emotionally separating himself from these very same companions. To Nora he painted himself as their country's friendless literary martyr: "He was Irish, that is to say, he was false to me." And he vented his spleen in "The Holy Office," the satirical poem mentioned above, which he hoped to distribute upon his departure. (The printer wouldn't deliver the broadsheets until he was paid.) As opposed to the Bards of beauty, Joyce portrays himself as Catharsis Purgative, "the sewer of their clique."

> That they may dream their dreamy dreams
> I carry off their filthy streams ...
> Those souls that hate the strength that mine has

Steeled in the school of old Aquinas....
And though they spurn me from their door
My soul shall spurn them evermore.

The poet W. H. Auden in his elegy for Yeats writes, "Mad Ireland hurt you into poetry," and Joyce apparently needed to be hurt into exile.

Anticipating their life together, Joyce became increasingly impatient of exchanging letters with Nora. "How I detest these cold written words!" he writes. In early October arrived the words they had been awaiting—"Appointment Zurich Go Saturday." Some of Joyce's sisters helped Nora prepare for the trip, and Joyce made an eleventh-hour appeal to Starkey, the poet who had retrieved his trunk and whose father owned a pharmacy. Simply assuming Starkey was somehow remorseful about being unable to lend money, Joyce asked him to collect the following:

1 toothbrush and powder
1 nail brush
1 pair of black boots and any coat and vest you have to spare.

The couple boarded the boat separately, to prevent John Joyce from discovering his son was in fact eloping. Joyce must have been anxious at first, wondering if Nora would perhaps lose her courage at the last moment. But she was stronger than Eveline; for better or worse, her love had risen above that of her lover's literary creation. Nora, a country-girl from Galway, was no Dubliner. And thus Joyce departed from the North Wall, his beloved beside him now, wearing the borrowed black boots of a pharmacist's son.

"I HATE A DAMN SILLY SUN THAT MAKES MEN INTO BUTTER."

It is hard to imagine a more strained and stressful beginning to Joyce's and Nora's life together. In London he left her in a park for two hours while seeking Arthur Symons, whom he wished to speak to about getting *Chamber Music* published, but Symons was unavailable. Joyce also missed an opportunity to borrow more money, which precipitated their urgent progress to Paris. There Nora was left in another park, each time in fear she was being abandoned, as Joyce found former students and old friends. The doctor Joyce had barely known—the one who had fed him seven courses—proved unexpectedly generous, giving the couple (for whom he perhaps felt some pity) sixty francs to continue their journey. Despite his best efforts at a smooth arrival in Zurich, Joyce received shocking news—there was no teaching position there. In the uncertain week that followed, he somehow managed to write the eleventh chapter of *Stephen Hero*, and the couple consummated their elopement, leading Joyce to write his brother coyly, "elle est touchée."

He learned of a vacancy at the Berlitz school in Trieste, then an Austrian port on the Adriatic coast. He and Nora departed with their one suitcase between them. They arrived to further disappointment: no position after all. For the next week Joyce did what he did best—he borrowed money and moved almost daily—and with an occasional free moment wrote the story that would become "Clay" in *Dubliners*. The head of the school, Almidano Artifoni, decided to help, offering him a job in Pola, another port 150 miles farther south of Trieste, "down towards Turkey," as Joyce himself said.

They were none too impressed with their new home. Joyce found Pola to be "a naval Siberia" and Nora deemed it a "queer old place." She was anticipating a swift move to Paris once Joyce finished his book and got rich; to speed the process she began studying French. They adjusted well enough: Nora was soon making Turkish cigarettes, and Joyce showed his assimilation by ending his letters, "Addio." The Berlitz supervisor Alessandro Francini Bruni, along with his wife, became good and perhaps unsuspecting friends: by January the Irish couple had moved in with them. Joyce wished to learn Alessandro's pure Tuscan dialect, and he tickled his Florentine boss by proudly speaking the medieval Italian of Dante. (Joyce reveled in his polyglot surroundings, where Italian, German, and Serbo-Croatian were regularly spoken.)

By the beginning of the year Nora was pregnant, and signs of discontent began to arise. A December letter survives, perhaps one Joyce passed to Nora under a café table, that begins, "For God's sake do not let us be any way unhappy tonight." She was understandably homesick and often met disdainful stares in the streets. Joyce admitted to his Aunt Josephine of being "quickly disillusioned," and asked her to write a 'Don't-be-alarmed-my-dear' letter to Nora. He was also realizing more fully that Nora would never be his companion in the arts. His work, however, was going well. In January he sent four new chapters of *Stephen Hero* to Stanislaus and completed two more the following month.

Joyce's long, sad record of his trials with publishers had already begun. "I wish some damn fool would print my verses," he writes. He was exchanging his first letters with Grant Richards, a London publisher whose masterful procrastination would cause the author early heartache. But other things were brighter: he somehow secured a piano, which helped him pass the time, and under his new pork-pie hat was a head of curly hair (Nora's doing), two early signs of his longstanding penchant for dandyism. Finally, his wish to leave this "Catholic country with its hundred races and thousand languages" was answered in March, by a reassignment to Trieste. All along he had made it quite clear that Stanislaus was to give no one his address, no doubt embarrassed at where his "voluntary exile" had delivered him.

Much of the next decade they would spend in Trieste, a colorful city of Greeks, Jews, Turks, and Albanians famed for the white walls of Miramare Castle. The poet Rainer Maria Rilke was composing his *Duino Elegies* nearby and Ibsen had found the place beautiful (a good sign). The Eastern influences fascinated Joyce, and soon after arriving he attended a Greek Orthodox mass. He had reached chapter 21 of his "terrible opus" and was wondering if people would have the patience to read it. Of other work he was more confident: during the mass "it seemed to me that my story "The Sisters" was rather remarkable." Trieste's political atmosphere and the sympathies of his new boss Artifoni stirred his socialist commitments. Yet he never gave up his realism, nor could he afford to, defending his constant need to make money by remarking that he couldn't believe "any State requires my energy for the work I am at present engaged in."

At home Nora was struggling through her pregnancy, often staying in bed to endure the 100-degree weather. But at least they had a flat; their first landlady had evicted them because of the soon-to-be child. Their economic woes continued and certainly weren't alleviated by Joyce's regular drinking binges in the workers' cafés. His teaching was going well, but he soon complained of the school's "reign of terror" and found the entire operation petty.

Dublin was soon on Joyce's mind. Reviving old grudges, he finally succeeded in having "The Holy Office" printed and sent copies to his brother for distribution. Unsuccessful in repeated attempts to lure

Stanislaus to Trieste, in July Joyce suggested they all live in a small cottage outside Dublin. Stan was more of an atheist than his brother, but this plan might have restored even his belief in Purgatory!

One positive outcome of this homesickness was his feverish progress on *Dubliners*; "A Painful Case," "The Boarding House," and "Counterparts" had all been written by midsummer. Yet Joyce was craving a "boiled leg of mutton" and poor Nora could only speak thirty words of the Triestine dialect. (She was no longer studying French and "very helpless" according to her husband.) The birth of Giorgio Joyce, on July 27, 1905, prevented what might have been a quick end to their exile.

"Son born Jim" read the telegram to family, though Joyce's friend Cosgrave continued his malicious ways by misreporting, "Mother and bastard doing well." (In a letter to Joyce his good wishes—"Hope the B. is doing well."—still show a trace of his earlier tastelessness.) In Trieste the stories were coming at a prodigous rate: "Ivy Day in the Committee Room" in August, in September "An Encounter" and "A Mother," followed in October by "Araby" and "Grace."

Joyce's continuing homesickness, and perhaps the new experience of fatherhood, caused him to relax the satirical malice against his birthplace. He was arranging his stories so that they told the life of Dublin, and he found it odd that no artist had "given" the city to the world before. His host of questions sent to Stanislaus for verification reflects the meticulous realism found in *Dubliners* (e.g. "Can a priest be buried in a habit?" "Can a municipal election take place in October?"). In the same letter Joyce reveals a growing frustration: "For the love of the Lord Christ change my curse-o'-God state of affairs." Wishing for a reversal of fortune, he sent a dozen stories to Grant Richards, who was in the process of rejecting *Chamber Music*.

By this time Joyce had succeeded in luring his brother to Trieste, an overture he had made as early as 1904, soon after his own arrival. (He had encouraged Stanislaus with these tidbits for success: "grow a moustache, pretend to know everything, and dress magnificently.") Once Stanislaus agreed to come, Joyce became exultant, but his frenetic planning also suggested how threadbare his existence had become, as when he carefully advised his brother how to use the fewest possible words when he telegrammed his arrival. He arrived in late October, 1905, and took up immediate residence in the Joyce's flat. Appearing as a "brother's keeper" not a moment too soon, he learned quickly what his new existence would mainly entail: Joyce and Nora had one centesimo between them and needed money immediately. Stanislaus was soon teaching English like his brother, but most of his salary went to general "household expenses," and within a few weeks Joyce was signing the Berlitz paybook and taking his brother's wages himself, to simplify things. The older brother also "borrowed" a pair of pants from the younger, one of the many "trivial exploitations," as Richard Ellman calls them, which Stan nonetheless endured for a length of time that is hard to fathom.

Joyce's correspondence with Grant Richards, meanwhile, had taken a positive turn. This opportunistic author suggested how the timeliness of an Irish general election might boost sales of his book with its Dublin locale, and he also raised the possibility of an American edition, "where there are some fifteen millions of my countrymen." In February Richards accepted the book and inquired about its author. He learned that Joyce, presently employed to "teach young men of this city the English language as quickly as possible with no delays for elegance," hoped income from the book would "enable me to resume my interrupted life."

This desired resumption would remain a distant goal. Joyce had already sent for inclusion an additional story, "Two Gallants," to which Richards's printer promptly objected on moral grounds. Other demands for revision followed, causing Joyce to dismiss the printer's taste and accuse him of prudery. "A one-eyed printer! Why has he descended with his blue pencil, full of the Holy Ghost?" he asks. However discouraging, these lengthy censorship battles strengthened Joyce's resolve for the didactic aims of his stories; his composition of a chapter of "moral history" in its exact form, he explained grandiloquently to Richards, constitutes the first step towards spiritual liberation in his country.

The following June he would make concessions, despite worries that they would prevent the Irish people from "having one good look at themselves in my nicely polished looking-glass." Ireland, though, would get *no* look at itself in this particular fictional looking-glass for the foreseeable future, Richards having by that time moved on to new stalling tactics, including a request first for an "autobiographical novel" that would lead to a better reception subsequently of *Dubliners*. Joyce hopefully mentioned the 914 pages of *Stephen Hero*, but in reality this work was still shapeless and unpublishable. Furthermore, the recent rejections and complications had discouraged him from working further.

Although Stanislaus dutifully helped relieve financial tensions at home, Joyce began to resent the "pinch of responsibility" he represented. Stoic, solemn, and later fashioned as Shaun the Postman in *Finnegans Wake*, he naturally resented the expensive dinners out and drunken carousing of his elder brother, the jovially dissipated Shem the Penman. (Stan would later point out repeatedly that they could have lived off their two salaries quite comfortably if not for Joyce's spendthrift habits.)

In February 1906 the Francini-Brunis, now in Trieste, prolonged their discord by again arranging for the Joyces to share their flat. They were often shaken that spring by the furious arguments upstairs, and sometimes they begged Stanislaus to cease pummeling his drunken brother. Artifoni, the brothers' boss, warned that he couldn't support two English teachers during the slower summer months, and Joyce must have received this "bad" news with a secret relief. He scoured Rome's newspapers and soon obtained a job as a correspondence clerk. Leaving Stan to face his creditors, he packed up his family in late July, and traveled by train, boat, then train again to the great city of classical ruins and modern renegades.

The family first landed in Ancona, a "filthy hole" where Joyce managed the unenviable feat of being "thrice swindled" in an hour. Their trying voyage was an omen of greater setbacks and disappointments to come. Soon after his arrival he reported his first impressions to Stan: he had passed the house where the poet Shelley had written *The Cenci*. It was Joyce's lone inspirational literary sight, the kind of which fills the effusively voluminous letters of his predecessors and contemporaries. In the very next sentence he writes, "I think you would like Rome more than I. The Tiber frightens me." Elsewhere he was duly unimpressed: St. Peter's seemed no larger than London's St. Paul's, and the music within was "nothing much." He visited the Colisseum "looking at it all round gravely from a sense of duty," and here might reside one theory as to Joyce's disillusion in the Eternal City: he resented the traditional adoration it commanded. "But enough now of stupid monuments," he abruptly concludes to Stan. Unlike many of his peers, for whom the Roman landscape was animated by the ghostly heroes and events of their schoolboy reading, Joyce lamented not knowing more of

Roman history and decided it was too late to learn. His experience lay in the Roman Catholic Aquinas, not in Imperial Roman Augustus: "So let the ruins rot."

"The first thing I look for in a city is the café," he declared, and even in this category Rome dissatisfied Joyce, who settled for the Caffe Greco, haunt of other British visitors such as Byron and Thackeray. He would later complain of knowing no one in the city, a fact that certainly contributed to the malaise of this regular socialite. Nearly ever other area of his life was discouraging as well. His job at the bank proved long and tedious, involving the daily writing of some 200 rather dull bank letters, either in Italian or English. He worked 10 hours a day, and even more when he moonlighted as a tutor to gain some much-needed extra income. Of course he never had enough; his lifestyle and habits assured that he wouldn't. From the week of his arrival he begged his brother for financial help, which was usually offered grudgingly. He soon complained of "two great patches" on the seat of his trousers, worn thin by sitting long hours.

His home life was no better: he suffered from bad dreams, and in September Giorgio was struck in the face by "some hoarse whore of an Italian driving a cart at breakneck speed and flourishing his whip." (Otherwise their son was the only one who seemed to thrive in Rome, learning many Italian words and receiving the warm attention of passersby.) The Joyces moved from room to room at an alarmingly frequent rate, even for them. Joyce and Nora were used to sleeping separately, but in December they secured housing with only a single bed. He reported to Stan their crude form of birth control, lying "in opposite directions, the head of one towards the tail of the other," but it proved ineffective: soon Nora was pregnant again. To make matters worse, Joyce's publication stalemates were continuing, and he replied angrily to Stanislaus when encouraged to keep writing: "I have written quite enough and before I do any more in that line I must see some reason why—I am not a literary Jesus Christ."

This peevishness covers a bald vocational desperation. Alienated as he was by his surroundings, Joyce of course felt that Rome heightened this desperate feeling, but it paradoxically helped him reach (if uneventfully at first) a new creative plateau. His attacks on the city became both more vociferous and more comical. He spoke of the "lazy whores of priests" chanting at St. Peter's, then asked Stan quite innocently, "Would you like any picture postcards of Rome?" This tourist's inquiry aside, he was increasingly irritated by the "stupid foreigners" who drove up the prices, as well as with his fellow clerks, who always complained about their penises, anuses, or testicles, usually before "a quarter of nine." Clerkly culture he no doubt found disagreeable, and the long, sedentary hours were threatening "mental extinction." Soon his invective reached a sublime irony: having reported his constipation to his brother, he concluded one letter with an update that a purgative cost him one pound. "Viva l'Italia!" he wrote, in the great bitterness of a mock-joyful tone.

Opposed to the Roman arrogance he found all around him, and to which he felt prey, the neglected merits of his homeland began to take on a new value for Joyce. In a late September letter he expressed fears that he had been "uncessarily harsh" in *Dubliners*, reproducing none of the city's attraction, its "ingenuous insularity and its hospitality." He also praised its natural beauty. Within a week he sent Stanislaus a postcard announcing he had a new story for *Dubliners*, one about Mr. Hunter, the Dublin Jew who once led him home safely. In that postscript lies the genesis of *Ulysses*, one of the greatest novels of the century.

Joyce was soon asking his Aunt Josephine, his one regular Dublin correspondent, to send city chronicles and a variety of ephemera— "tram-tickets, advts, handbills, posters, papers, programmes, &c." Soon a Dublin map hung on his wall. He admitted to being "something of a maniac," but these materials allowed his imagination to return to a place he knew intimately, and to a welcome sense of omniscience compared with the "confusing" streets of Rome. It's no coincidence that Stephen has a "skeleton map of the city" in his mind as he strolls through *A Portrait*, and John Joyce once remarked that if his son were set down in the Sahara desert, he'd make a map of it.

During the next few months he mentioned his new story occasionally, before confessing in February that "Ulysses" had not progressed beyond the title. He had other stories in mind but complained his hands were too cold. (The Roman winter had set in.) But he did make progress with a certain story, one that similarly required, as Ellman says, "a more indulgent view of Ireland." Entitled "The Dead," its tone is more nuanced and sympathetic than any other tale in *Dubliners*. Its eventual position as the final story humanizes the collection and defends masterfully its highest literary claims.

Arthur Symons, meanwhile indefatigable in his assistance, helped Joyce finally find a publisher for *Chamber Music*: Elkin Matthews accepted it early in 1907. The author by now looked disparagingly on many of the lyrics, but this distance clarified his fictional advances. "A page of 'A Little Cloud' gives me more pleasure than all my verses," he writes, referring to the final story added to *Dubliners*. Although Joyce wouldn't make a cent from his poetry, its acceptance gave him a much needed sense of progress in the marketplace: "I don't like the book but I wish it were published and be damned to it."

In February 1907 a riot broke out at Dublin's Abbey Theatre. The performance of J. M. Synge's *The Playboy of the Western World* caused an intense protest, culminating in Yeats's successful confrontation of the mob. These two writers were doing everything Joyce had merely talked of—forcefully showing their countrymen Ireland's hard truths—and the contrast was not lost on the "voluntary exile." He felt like a man in a house, he wrote Stanislaus, "who hears a row in the street and voices he knows shouting but can't get out to see what the hell is going on." Rome's lively political scene first encouraged Joyce's earlier socialist sympathies. He was present for a socialist "congress" and excitedly reported each of three related bomb blasts, an example of Stanislaus's observation that his brother thrived on the "excitement of incident." But Dublin's homegrown theatre turmoil revealed the shallowness of these political interests.

Even Joyce's anti-church convictions suffered from this new apathy. In the fall he had referred to the cassock-clad Jesuits as "black lice" and darkly predicted a new Inquisition if the Church's power were restored. Usually, then, Joyce would have been at his vituperous best at a February memorial procession for his hero Giordano Bruno, the Inquisition victim whose statue had been erected in Campo di Fiori in 1889. Instead the event left him "quite cold." It also led to a self-appraisal: faded hat, borrowed cloak, dirty boots, unshaven—he condemned himself as a "horrible example of free thought." Indifference had arisen in him, but not the kind that reflects "artistic inclination." He was becoming wearied by his own difficult existence: "My mouth is full of decayed teeth and my soul of decayed ambitions."

His general resentment of Rome and Italy continued to grow. He dubbed Henry James's charming and civilized accounts of the city "teaslop" and hated that Italians had achieved such great art, dismissing their High Renaissance masterpieces as simple page illustrations from the New Testament. When Stan questioned his criticisms, Joyce irately responded, "What the hell else would I do?" He was heavily biased by his experiences, particularly the countless and humiliating moves with a crying baby in tow. In February they relocated to a room on the Corso, though Joyce groused that Nora would only be satisfied for a week. Once he sardonically compared himself to St. Joseph, seeking out shelter for his holy family among heartless innkeepers.

So disillusioned by his surroundings, Joyce's thoughts turned inward, and he found himself ruminating on the artist's perennial question, how to combine "the exercise of my art with a reasonably happy life." He came to discover that such a combination was impossible for him in Rome. He had written practically nothing since his arrival, but his mind was still abuzz: "Yet I have certain ideas I would like to give form to.... These ideas or instincts or intuitions or impulses may be purely personal." He needed to reclaim this personal element as a priority in his life. In mid-February he impulsively resigned from his bank job, looking forward to matching the "pastime" of his fellow clerks—to leaving Rome behind with a "breaking of wind reward."

Stanislaus strongly objected to this action and informed Joyce that no teaching job remained for him in Trieste, despite Artifoni's earlier promises. His brother reaffirmed his intention to leave, hinting that Byrne's earlier prophecy—that Joyce would become a drunkard—was perilously close to being fulfilled. He looked into a position in Marseilles, but none was available. He would return to Trieste then, and he celebrated his pending escape from the Eternal City by drinking with two postmen on the Pincio. Once drunk, he showed his final earnings a little too freely: his two companions followed him out of the café, then beat and robbed him. Joyce left Rome as ignominiously as when he arrived, and he seemed to realize his eventual fate by early December: "This city, I confess, beats me.... I think it is the stupidest old whore of a town ever I was in."

"I AM A JEALOUS, LONELY, DISSATISFIED, PROUD MAN."

Joyce's fortunes would change for the better, but not for seven trying years. And in the meantime, they would worsen. His immediate prospects once back in Trieste, however, were not nearly as bleak as first thought. His successful return, in the face of his brother's conventional wisdom, demonstrated a repeated ability to land—somehow, some way—on his feet. The Joyces again moved in with the Francini-Brunis, despite owing them money from their last tenancy, and Joyce quickly regained the support of his more prominent pupils, among them a count and a baron. Joyce would always enjoy the affection of the higher classes, perhaps because of his erudition or maybe the gallantry inherent in his temperament. (As Richard Ellman explains, "he did not really believe in the poverty in which he dwelt.")

Another friend, the elegant Venetian newspaper editor Robert Prezioso, hired Joyce to write some articles on Ireland's experience under England, a situation that paralleled Trieste's. "I may not be the Jesus Christ I once fondly imagined myself, but I think I must have a talent for journalism," he quipped, at once humbled and smug. He also lectured on "the gradual reawakening of the Irish conscience," delivered in an elegant Italian that was warmly received. His old boss Artifoni, who fearing Joyce's popularity had recently rehired him, was pleased by the publicity. Joyce also made amends with his father at this time, although the latter did not hide his disappointment in his son's elopement: "I saw a life of promise crossed and a future that might have been brilliant blasted in one breath."

As for his writing, even Joyce's successes were of little consolation. On the eve of *Chamber Music*'s publication, Stanislaus argued all night with his brother, who nearly cabled the publisher Elkin Matthews to halt the book's printing. His pursuit of new careers during the next year reflects a dissatisfaction with his creative and personal lives: he contacted the South African Colonisation Society, sought work at the British Civil Service, applied for a scholarship at his old university and for a teaching job in Florence, dreamt of selling Irish tweeds in Trieste, and of a long-deferred singing career.

Further quixotic vocational paths were prevented by his contacting rheumatic fever. He spent July and August in the hospital, during which time Nora gave birth to their second child, Lucia, on July 26 in the paupers' ward. Joyce's abrupt resignation at the school added to the new difficulties of home life, but his slow recovery from the fever and the resulting free time permitted an important turn in his work. In September he finished "The Dead" and continued to develop the general plan for *Ulysses*. He also decided to rewrite the stalled *Stephen*

Hero as a shorter, five-chapter novel, *A Portrait of the Artist as a Young Man*; he finished the third chapter by the following April. *Dubliners*, however, continued to languish: Grant Richards had finally rejected it, and more recently three others had done likewise. In early 1908 the publishing house Maunsel & Co. requested it, but Joyce in his discouraged state did not get around to submitting it until the following year.

The Joyces by this time had rented two rooms with Stanislaus, which inevitably led to arguments: Nora was fed up with her husband, who was again drinking heavily, and both were frequently irritated with the disapproving Stanislaus. In May 1908 Joyce was stricken with iritis (an inflammation of the iris), the first of increasingly serious eye troubles that lay ahead. Nora suffered a miscarriage later that summer; Joyce morbidly pondered the fetus, mourning its "truncated existence." Their own existence seemed only slightly better: that fall Stanislaus noted sternly in his diary that he had saved his brother's family six times from starvation.

During a time of creative stagnation in early 1909, Joyce found much needed support in an unlikely place—Ettore Schmitz, a middle-aged manager of a paint company. He was a pupil of Joyce's, and after talking for a while about literature, he surprised his teacher by sheepishly admitting he had published two novels under the pseudonym Italo Svevo. Joyce was even more surprised by their subtle narratives, which would influence his own "interior monologues." Their relationship would be a rare, symbiotic one in Joyce's life: soon he had resumed *A Portrait* and finally sent *Dubliners* to the interested publisher. He also learned that a Belfast composer had set some of the *Chamber Music* poems to music, which gave him a more positive appraisal of his first book: "The book is in fact a suite of songs and if I were a musician I suppose I should have set them to music myself."

Stanislaus had recently suggested that he accompany Giorgio to visit family in Dublin, but in July Joyce, encouraged by an advance payment for English lessons, "bumped" his brother and traveled with Giorgio himself. The "voluntary exile" was returning home, and the next six weeks would be a tumultuous, defining time for Dublin's prodigal son. His family was happy to see them, though surprised "Stannie" wasn't present. Joyce's sister Eileen told him he looked "very foreign-looking." Joyce felt ambivalent about meeting his past friends, though in such an intimate city such occurrences were unavoidable. He regarded these as "mutual testings," and was guarded and aloof when visiting Gogarty at his expensive house. He questioned his friend's quieter, "man-of-standing" lifestyle, but gained new respect for Gogarty when he bluntly told Joyce, "I don't care a damn what you say of me so long as it is literature."

Joyce met Curran and found him unfriendly, though he enjoyed a warm reunion with Byrne. He frequently saw Cosgrave, who embittered by his own idleness, attempted to devestate his "friend" on August 6. He declared to Joyce that Nora had been unfaithful during their courtship, secretly meeting Cosgrave on her free nights. Joyce should have considered the dubious claim more carefully, but he instead seized on it. He had arrived in Dublin needful of finding betrayers among his friends, and now he could be Love's martyr, cuckolded by the Galway wife he once thought faithful. His fear of disloyalty had become a wish, springing from a strange part of his pysche that craved to be dominated and humiliated. "You stood with him: he put his arm around you and you lifted your face and kissed him," he writes Nora in a panic, outraged yet still curious for further detail. "What else did you do together?"

He asked Nora irrationally if Giorgio were truly his son. One easily feels most sympathy toward Nora, who must have been shocked by the allegations and perhaps fearful that it was a ruse by which Joyce could permanently desert her. She responded more with sadness than with the indignance the accusation merited. Stanislaus learned of the charges, and immediately he revealed a secret he had kept for several years: Cosgrave had confided in him long ago, admitting he had tried to steal Nora from Joyce but was rejected. This news confirmed the mistake Joyce already realized he had made, for in his distress he had walked to Byrne's house, at 7 Eccles Street, to seek comfort. Byrne relieved Joyce, suspecting long-anticipated treachery among Gogarty, Cosgrave, and others. Joyce happily believed him, and the rest is literary history: Byrne's house would be the Bloom's address in *Ulysses*, the home where Leopold (himself a cuckold) acts as a symbolic father to his newly found son Stephen, a modest Hamlet senior conversing with his junior.

A series of penitent letters, renewed in their passion, followed. Joyce had sent Nora "three enormous bags of shell cocoa," he wrote. "Make me worthy of you.... What can come between us now? We have suffered and been tried." He then took a promised trip to Galway, to introduce Giorgio to her family. The surroundings, full of traces of Nora's young womanhood, invested Joyce with an even greater ardor. He desired to be flogged by her, and his letters oscillated between the extremes of his visions: "One moment I see you like a virgin or madonna the next I see you shameless, insolent, half naked and obscene!" Before his return to Trieste Joyce purchased an expensive and rather ponderous necklace, with five dice on it and a tablet with his poem line, "Love is unhappy when love is away." He still had to await travel money from Stanislaus, who upon seeing the gift and its inscription dourly said, "So is love's brother."

Joyce stayed professionally busy during his six-week trip. He reviewed George Bernard Shaw's new play for *Il Piccolo della Sera*, Prezioso's paper, and subsequently used his press pass to haggle repeatedly for reduced train fare. More importantly, he met with George Roberts at Maunsel & Co. in mid-August, signing a new, more generous contract for the publication of *Dubliners*. He left in early September, with Giorgio and his sister Eva as well, and notified Stanislaus in Italian of their arrival and hardly surprising financial state: "*Pennilesse*."

The awkwardness caused by Joyce's and Nora's renewed passion quickly irritated Stanislaus, but an outburst was avoided by Joyce's unexpected second trip to Dublin, which came about by sheer chance: Eva quickly became homesick, but she did like one aspect of Trieste— the cinemas. Why didn't Dublin have any? Joyce was instantly inspired by the idea, and his excitement led four Triestine businessmen to finance his plans to bring a movie theater to "dear dirty Dublin." He checked in at Finn's Hotel, where Nora had worked, and put all his energy into the business venture, finding a location, furnishing it with potted palms and Windsor chairs. On Dec. 20, the Volta theater opened. Despite bad weather, it was well reviewed, but a maladroit choice of films and Joyce's return to Trieste ensured the theater's eventual failure.

Joyce and Nora's epistolary romance reached new heights (and plombed new depths) during this second visit. Once again Joyce alternated voices. Sometimes he sounded like the hopeful, Troubadour lover: "I know and feel that if I am to write anything fine or noble in the future I shall do so only by listening at the doors of your heart." While staying at the hotel he arranged to see the room where Nora once stayed, and like a pilgrim at a shrine laid his "errors and follies and sins and wondering and longing ... at the little bed in which a young girl had dreamed of me."

In other letters a more overheated, animal-like lover emerged, who addressed "My sweet little whorish Nora, ... dirty little girl." He was intent on baring his every fantasy in coarse, erotic terms. Nora gamely responded, which further kindled his arousal: "Tell me smallest things so long as they are obscene and secret and filthy," he begged. "Let every sentence be full of dirty immodest words and sounds," he asked of "my naughty wriggling little frigger." He wished for two beds for their "night-work" and longed to return to "my love, my life, my star, my little strange-eyed Ireland!" He did so in early January 1910, accompanied by another sister, Eileen.

A year later, this sister would retrieve the manuscript of *A Portrait* from the fire, where Joyce had tossed it during an argument with Nora. "There are pages here I could never have re-written," he told her gratefully once he had calmed himself. The incident suggests his despondent spirits. The past year had been a grim one—another move, supperless evenings, another eye malady, a fallout with Stanislaus. To make matters worse, he was enduring the all-too-familiar publishing complications with Maunsel & Co. George Roberts had gotten cold feet, and was now demanding certain passages be excised or edited. Joyce grew increasingly impatient with these objections. He responded to worries about a "George V" reference by writing the English king directly (!) to see if he minded the passage; he received a curt reply saying His Majesty did not express opinion on such cases. He went so far as to seek legal help, but he was advised against such action. Discouraged, he tied up the burnt pages of *A Portrait* and stored them in an old sheet.

Joyce's life and career reached a low point in 1912. Thirty years old, he was prepared to settle for a job teaching in Italian public school, but after traveling to Padua to take and pass the examinations, his Dublin degree was judged inadequate. Nora was eager to see her family again after eight years away. She departed with Lucia, but Joyce couldn't bear remaining behind. Begging some money from his pupil Schmitz, he and Giorgio followed after mother and daughter. Foolishly pushed into pleading his case at Maunsel & Co., Nora took along Joyce's father and his brother Jim. Unsurprisingly relations between the author and the alarmed George Roberts deteriorated further.

Joyce had proceeded onto Galway to meet Nora and her family, but a letter from Roberts, in which he proposed *another* change of publisher (Grant Richards), sparked Joyce's fiery return to Dublin. He retained legal counsel, an unfortunate choice in that he was poorly represented, and confronted Roberts by bringing along fellow writer Padraic Colum, who offered lukewarm support. Roberts, nearly fed up, curtly demanded that Joyce put forward a large sum of money to cover feared losses and libel law suits. Less unreasonably, Roberts on September 5 offered to sell Joyce the master sheets of *Dubliners* for thirty pounds. Joyce agreed, but he first talked Roberts out of one set of proofs. It was an incredibly fortunate acquisition, for the printer was less than accommodating. He steadfastly refused to release such unpatriotic pages, especially to their despicible author, so on September 11, he destroyed the master sheets. (Their fate—either by fire or by pulping—has remained unclear.) Joyce left Dublin—this time never to return—that very evening.

Before the family's train reached Munich, Joyce composed a valedictory satire, much like "The Holy Office" of eight years before. "Gas from a Burner" is spoken ironically in the voice of Roberts, who speaks of the country Joyce has just fled for good:

> But I owe a duty to Ireland:
> I hold her honour in my hand,
> This lovely land that always sent
> Her writers and artists to banishment
> And in a spirit of Irish fun
> Betrayed her own leaders, one by one.

After raising the specter of Parnell, Joyce vented his spleen with less savory lines, speaking as the faux-pious Roberts: "I'll penance do with farts and groans / Kneeling upon my marrowbones." Joyce's more lyrical "sensitive" poems have always seemed slight compared with his great accomplishments in prose, but the Irish Nobel Laureate Seamus Heaney correctly points to this pair of satirical broadsides as upholding a truly poetic energy—the couplets' "exact deadliness" in a language "with all the roused expectation of a loosed ferret." Joyce promptly had the attack printed and sent to Dublin where Charles, this time, served as messenger. (John Joyce was angered by the diatribe, finding it unbecoming a gentleman.)

Even under the worst circumstances, Joyce nevertheless retained a certain aristocratic flair. He seemed the "Gracehoper" mentioned in *Finnegans Wake*: glibly evading debts, relying on Stanislaus's paychecks interest- and conscience-free, and yet managing to pay for the restoration and safe shipment of the Joyce family portraits. These heirlooms arrived in Trieste in the spring of 1913, and the author would haul them around Europe for the rest of his life. Soon his job prospects improved. He secured a more respectable teaching job at the Scuola Superiore, which in turn augmented his reputation as a private tutor. During the lessons he most enjoyed talking about matters interesting to him. (To a lawyer Joyce dismissed Freud and praised Giambattista Vico, a philosopher whose theories of history would influence the structure of his later novels.)

At times he taught more eccentrically, as when he challenged one pupil to the highest ballerina's kick. (Thanks to his gangly body, he won.) His less conventional style encouraged a more personal interest in his student Amalia Popper, the daughter of a Jewish businessman. Creatively Joyce returned to older forms, writing several poems that would appear later in *Pomes Penyeach*. The young lover's adoration had resurfaced, though this time tempered by the elder's irony and self-deprecation. This mix lends intrigue to the epiphany-like entries of *Giacomo Joyce*:

> A flower given by her to my daughter: frail gift, frail giver, frail blue-veined child.
>
> My words in her mind: cold, polished stones sinking through a quagmire.

The first example has the same tender perception of the poems, and in fact Joyce also put the sentence into verse form. The second is sharper in tone, more befitting a notebook whose title compares its author (unfavorably) with the famed lover, Giacomo Casanova. Joyce's writing resumed, but his obscurity continued, his work destined for yet another notebook.

His publication fortunes were finally about to change, with the unexpected arrival of two letters in late 1913. The first was from Grant Richards. He regretted his earlier treatment of Joyce and wished to consider *Dubliners* again. The second was from Ezra Pound, literary ideologue and tireless publicizer of new writers and movements. Pound was serving as Yeats's secretary and contacted Joyce at his suggestion, hearing they "had a hate or two in common." He introduced Joyce to a few literary journals he represented, which published "markedly modern" stuff, and welcomed him to submit material. Before receiving a first reply, Pound wrote again with a flattering update: Yeats had retrieved Joyce's poem "I Hear an Army," which Pound wanted to include in his anthology *Des Imagistes*. And contributors were paid.

Joyce hardly needed further encouragement—without delay he sent Pound *Dubliners* and the newly revised first chapter of *A Portrait*. Pound liked what he read, and results came swiftly. H. L. Mencken accepted three *Dubliners* stories for the American magazine *The Smart Set*, and a London periodical, *The Egoist*, began printing *A Portrait* in serial format on Feb. 2, 1914, Joyce's birthday (a coincidence that pleased him). A week earlier Richards agreed to publish *Dubliners*; perhaps the flurry of attention Joyce was receiving instilled him with new resolve. The book finally appeared in June, and Pound hailed it as symbolizing a "return to style in English prose."

The serialization of *A Portrait* provided income and spurred Joyce forward: he sent the third chapter to Pound in July, and despite the complications of World War I—the isolation of Austrian-ruled Trieste and the resulting postal disruption—Pound safely received the final two chapters by August 1915. He thought it splendid, and Joyce was also encouraged by his editor at *The Egoist*, Harriet Shaw Weaver. When five publishers rejected *A Portrait* in novel form, she generously agreed to print it herself, and a New York publisher, B.W. Heubsch, was also impressed enough to venture American publication. He received advances from both. After such delay, discouragement, and manipulation at the hands of earlier publishers, Pound's celerity, Weaver's support, and Huebsch's straight talk must have made Joyce unspeakably happy. Enjoying a devoted and intelligent readership at last, he seemed to write endlessly, composing his three-act play, *Exiles*, and making headway on the first chapters of *Ulysses*.

The war worsened in 1915. In January Stanislaus, outspoken in his pro-Italian and anti-imperial sympathies, was confined to an Austrian internment camp. More shrewd in his criticisms, Joyce remained free, and their sister Eileen married a Czech bank cashier in April. (With typical linguistic fascination, he informed them that "Joyce" in Czech meant "eggs," which he deemed a fair portent for a large family!) Italy's declaration of war in May didn't shake Joyce's political apathy in the least, but he did realize his adopted city was increasingly under siege.

Eileen and her husband traveled to Prague, and the Joyces secured passports and began the anxious task of avoiding internment and departing Trieste. Joyce's many years of teaching yielded at this moment of crisis a veritable regiment of guardian angels. His more prominent pupils assuaged the Austrian authorities, who subsequently permitted the Joyces passage. Once on a train bound for Switzerland, Joyce was greeted by a Greek pupil, and among the officers was yet another student, who chose not to intimidate the family with baggage searches. They arrived safely in Switzerland and settled in Zurich. Joyce explained his residence in a letter, saying "it is the first big city after the frontier," yet perhaps the last place one might have expected to attract him—a neutral city.

"I HOPE THAT NOW MATTERS MAY BEGIN TO GO A LITTLE MORE SMOOTHLY FOR ME."

Joyce spent eleven years in Trieste, which he came to consider his "second country." Consequently the move to Zurich proved difficult at first. The family moved with their typical, disorienting frequency, finally staying for nearly a year in a "stuffy and small" flat they increasingly disliked. At home they continued to speak Triestine Italian. Nora was depressed by the German spoken around her, and the language barrier caused the children to fall behind in school. The cost of moving necessitated financial help from Nora's uncle; fortunately further assistance was forthcoming. With Yeats's support, Joyce was awarded a grant by the Royal Literary Fund, and Pound diligently helped find other such sources of literary compensation in the coming months.

These awards not only relieved financial hardships, but the recognition they implied also encouraged the author in his work. He now had the luxury of approaching it on his schedule: he'd sleep late, work on *Ulysses* in the afternoons, then discuss ideas for the book at various cafés late into the night. Despite the sublimity of his "standing alone," Joyce's garrulous demeanor quickly earned him many friends in a city enlivened by diverse refugees. He frequented the Café Voltaire, whose customers Tristan, Tzara, and Hans Arp conceived the Dada movement, and the Café Odéon, where Joyce may have met Lenin, a regular before leaving for a prior engagement—the Russian Revolution.

Joyce continued to tutor privately, although some pupils offered him subtle support by paying for lessons and never taking them. One friend recalls him being "humorously indignant" if he sometimes actually had to give the paid-for lesson. Even then, he couldn't clear *Ulysses* from his mind; he would read pages to students and discuss its themes. One student asked if there were enough words for him in English. "Yes," he replied cryptically, "there are enough, but they aren't the right ones." He desired a pre-lingual language that was above all languages: the interior monologues of *Ulysses*, his day-book, approach this goal, but he wouldn't reach it till his "book of the night," *Finnegans Wake*.

Meanwhile, Harriet Weaver was attempting to publish *A Portrait* but faced the same frustration with printers as before. Exasperated, Joyce proposed a complex plan where offending passages would be typed and individually pasted into printed-but-censored copies. Fortunately he didn't have to resort to this. His American publisher Heubsch agreed to print the sheets in New York and send them to London afterward. In December 1916 Heubsch published the American edition of *Dubliners* and the premiere edition of *A Portrait of the Artist as a Young Man*. (Joyce insisted the latter book feature a 1916 date, for he felt it had been a lucky year for him.)

Joyce's eye troubles returned in early February 1917. Suffering from glaucoma and other retinal afflictions, he ceased working. The resulting despondency, however, was somewhat lessened by mysteriously good news later in the month: an "unknown and generous benefactor" announced that Joyce would receive a regular gift of 50 pounds: "but for it I should be in the poorhouse," he thankfully informed Pound. He would discover only later that his patron was none other than Weaver, who at the same time was publishing the first English edition of *A Portrait*.

In the fall the family temporarily moved to Locarno, in the Italian Swiss Alps, to escape the "infamous weather" of Zurich. Joyce's doctor had advised the change, though the author, convalescent from eye surgery, soon found the scenic location rather too quiet compared with the city. He did meet there a young doctor, Gertrude Kaempffer, who had recently recovered from tuberculosis in Locarno's more favorable climate. Joyce was instantly infatuated with this reticent woman, secretly writing her letters about his first sexual experience and indiscreetly propositioning her. Embarrassed, she refused. The incident suggests the intensity with which Joyce was converting his experiences, however brief, into mythic occasions in *Ulysses*. His attempted affair, for example, inspires Leopold Bloom's secret letters, which he signs "Henry Flower," and the "Nausicaa" episode, where the real-life Gertrude becomes the Irish lass, Gerty MacDowell.

Joyce had entered an obsessive stage regarding his work: "I write and I think and write and think all day and part of the night." He would begin with a list of phrases and then draft an episode with them, as if constructing a narrative with scraps of a prose poem. Aside from the "interior monologue" viewpoint mentioned above, Joyce's other innovation was structural—a pairing of mythic detail with the narrative events of his novel, "a continuous parallel between contemporaneity and antiquity," as the American poet T. S. Eliot influentially defined it, done with such scrutiny and consistency as to be a "scientific discovery." Describing this application of Homer's *Odyssey* and its hero Ulysses to his modern Irish setting, he happily wrote Pound in July about "my Ulysses born anew / In Dublin as an Irish jew."

By the fall he completed the first three books or *Telemachiad*, named after the first section of Homer's epic and featuring Ulysses's son, Telemachus. He sent the manuscript to a friend, who managed to borrow a typewriter and was willing to type the difficult text. Joyce's habits of revision further complicated this task: he jotted notes on dozens of scraps of paper throughout his day and during conversations, then returned to his flat late at night to read them with a magnifying glass. Afterward he would send revision requests, which often served to lengthen the original work substantially. The winter in Locarno was less mild than expected, and after three months the Joyces returned to Zurich. ("Jim never spoke a word to me," Nora complained, relieved to be back among friends.)

Pound was highly impressed with the beginning of *Ulysses*, writing to the author in his mock-American dialect, "I recon you're a damn fine writer, that's what I recon." Now associated with a more avant-garde magazine in America, *The Little Review*, Pound asked its editors if they would consider publishing these chapters in serial form. One editor, Margaret Anderson, was immediately struck by the opening of the third chapter, "Proteus":

Ineluctable modality of the visible: at least that if no more,
thought through my eyes. Signatures of all things I am here
to read, seaspawn and seawrack, the nearing tide, that rusty
boot. Snotgreen, bluesilver, rust: coloured signs.

The beauty of the prose stunned her. "We'll print it if it's the last
effort of our lives," she vowed. The first excerpt appeared in the March
1918 issue, and it nearly *would* be their last effort: their ensuing struggles
with censors would make *Ulysses* a famous, scandalous book in America.

Joyce received more good news in Zurich—he was the beneficiary
of another monetary gift, this one from a local patroness. Surprisingly
solvent, he was convinced by a friend to invest in an English-language
drama troupe. This investment became one of the more humorous and
lively of his recent enterprises. Deciding to produce Wilde's *The
Importance of Being Earnest*, they gained the British-consulate's approval
by implying a certain patriotic aim behind their actions. Joyce recruited
a handsome young man from the consulate office, Henry Carr, to play
the lead role, a disastrous choice in hindsight. The English Players, as
they called themselves, enjoyed a successful opening night on April 29,
but Carr was miffed at receiving only 10 francs, the agreed payment for
amateurs. He also demanded 150 francs for the cost of a dapper outfit
he purchased for the production.

Joyce, always keen to hear of treachery, angrily confronted him at
the consulate's. An argument erupted, with Carr threateningly calling
Joyce a "cad" and a "swindler." Morally offended, the latter's litigious
spirit took over, and soon he slapped Carr with two lawsuits, one for the
payment of tickets Carr had sold, the other for libel. He eventually won
the first case, which filled him with joy. It was a victory against all British
authority and inspired him to write a pub song, thoroughly Irish and
derisive, in celebration. He at first refused to drop the libel case, upon
his lawyer's advice, and would pay for his stubbornness the following
year, when Carr won his countersuit. Overall, his losses proved greater
than his earnings.

The English Players had a brief but successful life, performing
Synge's *Riders to the Sea* (featuring first-time actress Nora in a role
perfect for a Galway girl) and Shaw's controversial *Mrs. Warren's
Profession*, then banned in England. Still tainted by the fight with Carr,
Joyce smartly separated himself from the troupe, but without his energy

it eventually folded. The English playwright Tom Stoppard wonderfully commemorates this theatrical (mis)adventure in *Travesties*. Joyce is a prominent character, and in one parodic scene he dictates parts of *Ulysses* in the Zurich Library:

> JOYCE: Send us bright one, light one, Horhorn, quickening and wombfruit.
> GWEN: Send us bright one, light one, Horhorn, quickening and wombfruit.
> JOYCE: Thrice.
> GWEN: Uh-hum.
> JOYCE: Hoopsa, boyaboy, hoopsa!
> GWEN: Hoopsa, boyaboy, hoopsa!
> JOYCE: Hoopsa, boyaboy, hoopsa!
> GWEN: Likewise thrice?
> JOYCE: Uh-hum.

Joyce maintained his creative energy despite further bouts of irritis. His play *Exiles* was published by Grant Richards on May 25, 1918, and the American serialization of *Ulysses* held him to a productive pace. Weaver meanwhile attempted to arrange an English serialization in *The Egoist*, but once again she could find no willing printer. She even approached Leonard and Virginia Woolf, who had recently founded their Hogarth Press. They denied having the capacity for such a project, and in any case they found the latest episode—with its Irish-Jewish canvasser eating a kidney and moving his bowels—to be "underbred." Leopold Bloom would share only his name with London's exclusive Bloomsbury group.

Joyce now befriended Frank Budgen, a thoughtful young English painter who would later write an important early book on *Ulysses*—part criticism and part memoir—during Joyce's lifetime. The pair was soon inseparable: they drank until dawn and Joyce would break out with a "spider dance"—long limbs flying everywhere—on the trendy Bahnhofstrasse! He found in Budgen an admirer with whom he could talk through the complexities of *Ulysses*, but also a confidant who didn't shy away from arguments. One night at a restaurant Budgen suggested his friend underestimated the importance of Freud and psychoanalysis. Joyce welcomed the chance to quarrel. "Why all this fuss and bother about the mystery of the unconscious?" he countered. "What about the mystery of the conscious? What do they know about that?"

By this time Joyce was articulating the various *schema* of his novel: its eighteen chapters will take the characters through the eighteen hours of June 16, 1904; in each an organ of the body will subtly reappear throughout, becoming a literary version of the musical "leitmotif" employed by the composer Wagner, an early influence on Joyce. Budgen became a witness to the working out of a masterpiece, written by a man who once said he'd make a good grocer's assistant because of his attention to detail: "I can testify that no line ever left his workshop without having been the object of a hundredfold scrutiny."

To Budgen, Joyce often defended his estimation of Homer's Ulysses as the most complete man—a son, father, husband, lover, soldier, trickster, king, and revenger. Budgen mentioned Jesus instead, but Joyce rejected the comparison: "He was a bachelor, and never lived with a woman. Surely living with a woman is one of the most difficult things a man has to do, and he never did it." Such a comment reflected his continuing troubles with Nora, who endured his unusual hours and frenetic fits of work, despite finding the pages of *Ulysses* he read her mainly distasteful. One night, irritated at her husband's drunkenness, she informed him she had disposed of his manuscript. He sobered immediately, shell-shocked, till she admitted her ruse.

Once she tearfully admitted to Budgen that Joyce wished to see her with other men, so that he could write about his anguish. He probably hoped to identify better with Leopold Bloom; significantly, he had also pursued this desire once before in Trieste. There, he encouraged a liason between Nora and their friend Robert Prezioso before being repulsed by the possible consequences: he ended his machinations by confronting the manipulated Prezioso, to his friend's great shame. Soon after the Armistice was signed on November 11, 1918, thus ending the war, he turned his erotic interest outward, in a way that threatened him less than a possible indiscretion by his wife.

Looking out his window on the Universitätstrasse one day, he spied a woman in the neighboring building. She was pulling a toilet chain. Soon he passed her in the street, and the sight of her face enraptured him: he imagined her as the young girl whom he saw in 1898 on the shore of the Irish Sea, lifting her skirts, now come to him again. He soon learned her name was Marthe Fleischmann, and another clandestine correspondence ensued. Their letters quickly became risqué, Joyce asking her about women's "drawers." (Joyce had a longtime fascination with women's underwear; he kept a pair of doll's panties in his pocket, often providing café entertainment by putting two fingers in them and walking his hand seductively toward a friend!)

A strange meeting took place on February 2, 1919, Joyce's birthday and also Candlemas Day. Joyce prepared the studio of Budgen's, who was rather uneasy about the rendezvous, and borrowed a large Chanukah candle to set the mood. Returning the candle later, he sheepishly said it was used for a "black mass." Whatever occurred, Fleischmann was the latest object of the author's periodical burst of adoration mixed with lechery. The experience is echoed in *Ulysses* in the characters of Martha Clifford (Bloom's amorous correspondent) and Gerty McDowell (the object of Bloom's voyeurism, a tendency shared by both Joyce and his later creation Earwicker in *Finnegans Wake*).

Joyce's sister Eileen and her husband moved back to Trieste after the war, and soon he was contemplating a return as well. His relocations always resulted from a need to escape—from the trials and disappointments of one city to the freedom and promise of the next. If he were looking for propelling circumstances, he did not (as usual) need to look far. In August *Exiles* was finally staged in Munich, but the reviews were mixed at best, with one article speaking of an "Irish stew." The author himself flatly pronounced it a "flop." He was more disturbed, however, by the puzzled and worried responses he was receiving to his latest *Ulysses* chapter, "Sirens." And the writing itself exhausted him: he often worked sixteen or more hours a day, with heaps of notes and drafts scattered across two beds.

The "sandblast" of composition tired him mentally as well. Each episode, which by now had also been assigned a peculiar liberal art, left behind it a "burnt up field" of what had once been an interest of Joyce's. After completing the fugue-structured "Sirens," he complained that he could no longer listen to music: "I see through all the tricks and can't enjoy it any more." Such a statement speaks to the encyclopedic ambitions the author held for his *Ulysses*. A final setback precipitated his return to Trieste. In October his local patroness (the daughter of John D. Rockefeller, as it turned out) abruptly terminated her financial support. She may have been angered by Joyce's steadfast refusal to be analyzed by Carl Jung, another beneficiary of her generosity. In any case, her decision reduced Joyce's income substantially. The higher life he had enjoyed in Zurich abruptly came to an end. The Joyces returned to Trieste later that month.

Much changed by the war, Trieste did not provide the homecoming Joyce expected. Costs in the city had risen dramatically, 8 to 10 times by his own estimation. He resumed teaching at the Scuola (recently renamed the University of Trieste) but—his mind completely absorbed by his creative work—he found the job even more distasteful than before. His residence with his sister's family was a delicate balance at best, and Stanislaus had changed too. More confident and having his own friends, the changes were entirely for his good, but they nevertheless vexed his older brother. Stan also felt bitterness toward Joyce—for his ingratitude at his sacrifices generally and specifically because *Dubliners* had not been dedicated to him, despite an earlier promise. He also showed no sympathy toward Joyce's more radical writing styles, which likely irritated Joyce most. He defended his work, calling these "innocent pages" the only repayment he could offer for his brother's financial "investments."

Joyce's Triestine friends believed him a different person, and the huge book he was writing explained this difference, a new reticence that would grow throughout his later years. In November he began "Nausicaa" with its "namby-pamby jammy marmalady drawsery" style, which he mimicked from the four romance novels and penny hymnbook begged from Aunt Josephine back in Dublin. He completed it by his birthday (always a good omen for Joyce) and soon restored editor Harriet Weaver's faith in his durable powers. She thought him "medicinal" for being "so unflattering to our human nature." He had something of both the doctor and priest in him, she concluded, to which he jovially brought up his false starts in medical school, saying he would have been "even more disastrous to society at large" had he continued. Unsurprisingly he corresponded often with Frank Budgen, the one friend whose feedback he valued, begging him to come to Trieste and explaining his next chapter, the chronicle of prose styles mentioned earlier, in exhaustive detail.

He told Pound seven months after his arrival that he had not spoken 100 words to anyone, memorably expressing his cloistered determination: "I must finish my book in quiet even if I sell off the furniture I have here." Pound was residing in Venice by May 1920, and

he initiated an overdue meeting, which took place the following month
in nearby Sermione. He once again served Joyce at a critical time,
listening to his dissatisfied friend's vague plans before suggesting
something better: Joyce would move to London, with a week's stay in
Paris on the way; Pound would ease the relocation by arranging contacts
and accommodations during the stopover. The Joyces' week in Paris
turned into a 20-year-residence. During their visit Pound gave Joyce a
pair of boots and a suit and altered his life forever.

"Is it possible that I am worth something?"

Joyce's twenty years in Paris were by far the longest of the many stages
of his exile. He arrived on July 8, 1920, to find his reputation had
preceded him. This reception in the most literary of cities must have
been deeply gratifying, but he responded by retreating from it,
exhibiting what Richard Ellman calls a more "somber, restrained
manner." During his first two years in Paris he completed *Ulysses* in a
frenzied fashion, and its publication led to a greater frenzy, both locally
and internationally. Yet there was no grand return to the hijinks and
anecdotes of his earlier days. He lost himself in an even more demanding
project, *Finnegans Wake*, a universal, pre-linguistic, synchronistic myth
requiring at once the broadest of erudition and the most painstaking
poetic attention. (A pair of critical opinions—that one must know 17
languages to appreciate the *Wake* and that it represents the "splitting of
the linguistic atom"—together suggest this dual demand.) In his
personal life he became something strangely (for him) like a stable family
man, frequenting the same restaurants with Nora and the children and
surrounding himself with a circle of devoted, trusted admirers.

Pound continued to be the most dedicated of this circle. In his role
of harbinger he distributed copies of *A Portrait*, praised its author
effusively, and arranged for a French translation. He ensured Joyce's
arrival would draw attention, and Joyce let his friend do the talking for
him as he completed the "Circe" chapter in December, moving on to last
three episodes. He soon met and won the support of two bookstore
proprietors and fixtures of Parisian literary life, Adrienne Monnier and
Sylvia Beach. Joyce visited the latter's English-language shop
Shakespeare and Company, a headquarters for poor expatriate writers.
He borrowed books from its lending library, much like he borrowed

more everyday things—beds and writing desks—from other acquaintances willing to indulge him his needs and complaints.

During the holidays Joyce met the influential Paris writer Valery Larbaud, who soon was "raving mad" about *Ulysses*, calling it as "great and comprehensive and human as Rabélais," the premiere French writer of the Renaissance. Joyce was nearing the end of his book by the spring. He begged his old friend Ettore Schmitz to bring him a suitcase he had left in Trieste, in which he had "lodged the written symbols of the languid sparks which flashed at times across my soul." These were notes for the final two chapters, "Ithaca" and "Penelope," the first sentence of which would contain 2500 words. In the meantime the American editors of *The Little Review* were on trial for publishing obscenity, found in four chapters of Joyce's novel. They were defended by New York attorney John Quinn, who for some time supported Modernist writers, Joyce included, by purchasing manuscripts of their works. The editors were found guilty and fined fifty dollars. Interest among publishers consequently cooled, and Joyce despaired of the book ever seeing print.

His friendship with Sylvia Beach then became instrumental: she asked if Shakespeare and Company could have the honor of publishing *Ulysses*, a proposal to which Joyce immediately agreed. Beach would publish 1,000 copies and advertise its long-anticipated appearance. (Winston Churchill was among the advance subscribers.) The author would receive 66% of the royalties, an outrageously generous amount. Weaver quickly made plans to borrow Beach's master sheets for an English edition, thus circumventing the squeamish printers who had so delayed *A Portrait*'s publication. Joyce, however, still endured unexpected censorship: one typist, recruited by Beach to finish "Circe," left her work in plain view; her husband read it and angrily threw it into the fire. Joyce had to rewrite that section, with the help of an earlier copy returned to him from New York.

Joyce did find the time to meet many of Paris's literary luminaries, or those paying their respectful visits from London. Monnier introduced him to her friends André Gide and Paul Valéry, he dined one night with Wyndham Lewis and T. S. Eliot, who would soon complete his famous poem *The Waste Land*, and his encounter with Marcel Proust, Paris's other novelist-genius, instantly generated a flock of apocryphal anecdotes. Each was diffident toward the other, though Joyce did attend Proust's funeral the following year. Other exotic rumors surrounded him: he was an Austrian or British spy; he was a cocaine addict (he sometimes took the drug for his painful eye inflammations); he wore black gloves to bed; he was the founder of dadaism (a confused association from his Zurich days), etc.

His personal life was far less glamorous: the Joyces continued moving from one place to the next, becoming swiftly disenchanted with this "matchbox" or that "damned brothel." Joyce's growing recognition further encouraged his natural extravagance, so the family's financial situation remained constantly precarious, despite book advances and Weaver's unflagging generosity. (One modern estimate has her total gifts equaling some million dollars.) He also occasionally reverted to his earlier drunken days, holding court with Larbaud or Lewis at the Gypsy Bar near the Panthéon. When especially drunk he would recite Verlaine or Dante, which earned him the nickname "le poète."

Joyce suffered further attacks of iritis during this final, exhausting stretch of composition. He described to Weaver how he worked for twelve hours and then stopped for five minutes "when I can't see anymore." The book, more than ever, risked leaving its author a broken man. His head was full of "pebbles and rubbish and broken matches and lots of glass," he said. Elsewhere he complained of his head reeling, but added mischievously, "that is nothing compared with the reeling of my readers' brains." Descriptions of *Ulysses* were often self-deprecating; he would cleverly speak of his "uselessly unreadable Blue Book of Eccles" in *Finnegans Wake*. A young Irishman named Arthur Powers began visiting Joyce. He cheered the author and accompanied him on long walks along the Champs-Élysées and the Seine, an enforced break from writing. Joyce often determined how poor his eyesight was by counting the lights on the Place de la Concorde.

Reading proof sheets during the summer and fall, Joyce often expanded the text dramatically. He thought the many additional details improved the characters' interior monologues, but the many changes understandably distressed the Dijon printer, who nonetheless reset the book as the author wished. He announced on October 29 that his "epic of two races (Israelite-Irish)" was complete, though his revision of the last four episodes continued until the new year. On December 7 Larbaud gave a much-publicized lecture on Joyce's ambitious, difficult novel. He was supplied with a complex schematic chart of each chapter's several characteristics, "in order to help him to confuse the audience a little more," as Joyce joked. In truth he was forever proud of the novel's unparalleled structural complexity, defending its mysteries to a translator:

> If I gave it all up immediately, I'd lose my immortality. I've put in so many enigmas and puzzles that it will keep the professors busy for centuries arguing over what I meant, and that's the only way of insuring one's immortality.

There were 250 admirers present at the event, which also featured a reading of passages translated into French and an American actor demonstrating the rhythms of the original. Larbaud's enthusiastic lecture summarized Joyce's earlier work, demonstrated the schematic organization of *Ulysses*'s episodes, and defended both Bloom's Jewishness and the "vulgarity" of the novel, saying of the latter that man's lower functions could not be excluded from a book about "the whole man." After much applause, Joyce (who had hidden behind a screen) came forward blushing, accepting the acclaim for his seven years of hard work, the "foolish author of a wise book."

Joyce received the first copy of *Ulysses* on his birthday—February 2, 1922. Beach, sensitive to the author's superstitions, ensured its on-time arrival by arranging for a train conductor from Dijon to deliver it to Paris personally. After dinner that night Joyce proudly presented the book to his friends. Visually the book was printed to his specifications, white letters on a blue cover, symbolizing Homer and the white islands of Greece shining on the sea. The author of *Ulysses* was 40 years old. "They are all there, the great talkers, they and the things they forgot," he said of his novel, and its publication spurred a new wave of great talkers, everyone being eager to "weigh in" on this literary event.

Larbaud said *Ulysses* marked Ireland's sensational return into the best European literature, and Yeats judged it "an entirely new thing," the product of a "playful mind like a great soft tiger cat." Ernest Hemingway, who recalled in his memoir *A Moveable Feast* that "in those days there was no money to buy books," at least found some means in this case—"Joyce has a most goddamn wonderful book," he crowed. Others were more ambivalent. George Bernard Shaw thought it "hideously real," and the book made him appreciate anew his own escape from Dublin as a young man. He declined to subscribe which earned Pound's scorn. And others were less than impressed. George Moore, Joyce's earliest supporter, thought he had "gone to seed," and the influential Catholic writer Paul Claudel, who saw in the novel merely the "hatred of the renegade," returned his inscribed copy. Neither Joyce's father nor Aunt Josephine found the book very appealing; his aunt thought it "not fit to read." Joyce was firm in his response: "If *Ulysses* isn't fit to read, life isn't fit to live."

A host of disappointments followed his triumphant completion of *Ulysses*. First, Nora was characteristically unimpressed with her husband's literary work. She offered to sell her copy to Powers, and never had enough interest to read it, despite his repeated requests. Nora wished for them to visit Ireland again, so that the children could see their grandparents. Joyce resisted, marveling at the creation of the Irish Free State but fearing even more the likely instability. After an April quarrel, Nora departed with the children. (They were indeed endangered while in Galway, caught amid the violence of the civil war, forced to flee the city by train as the Free State soldiers and the Irish Republican Army clashed.) "I am a man looking into a dark pool," he writes plaintively to his wife in Galway, or, as he says in the *Wake*, "Loonely in me loneness."

For a man of his reputation and accomplishment, he still frequently appeared down on his luck. He asked for a new necktie from an American friend and didn't hesitate begging a new pair of socks— from his taxi driver! Even devotees such as Beach were beginning to tire of Joyce's constant neediness. Pushed to arrange further reviews and raise subscriptions, she finally said she was not interested in "hustling to boom the book." Joyce's children also became a sorrow to him: restless, Giorgio held an uninspiring bank job, much like his father before him. Lucia, affected by her nomadic life, jumped unhappily from school to school. From 1920 she had begun to exhibit signs of schizophrenia.

In *Ulysses* Joyce describes Paris "rawly waking, crude sunlight on her lemon streets ..." It was an earlier man's observation, one which he was increasingly incapable of making. Soon after the novel's publication his eye troubles grew worse: "I always have the impression that it is evening," he told one friend. In search of doctor's opinions, or second opinions, or a climate that might improve his condition naturally, Joyce stayed temporarily in London, Marseilles, and Nice, where he also had 17 rotten teeth pulled. By the following June he had had three operations, which led to his wearing a patch over his left eye. Joyce was quite similar to Lucia in being vulnerable to mental illness, but he could always find refuge within the life and humor of his literary creations. And so, beset with personal disappointment and worsening eyesight, he began to imagine his next, and final, book.

Laboriously composed for 16 years, *Finnegans Wake* wasn't published till 1939, just a few years before its author's death. Joyce began writing in March 1923, referring to it in a letter to Weaver as a "universal history." He conceived the book as a dream of the legendary hero Finn MacCumhal, dying next to the River Liffey. Finn dreamt of Humphrey Chimpden Earwicker, his wife Anna Livia, their twins Shem and Shaun, and their sister Isabel. These characters, existing in a true "fluid succession of presents" that span the world and level its long history into one plane, serve as archetypes that represent Everymen and more. Thus Shem and Shaun find their biblical parallels in Cain and Abel and expand further in Joyce's imagination as old Nick and Saint Mick. Earwicker is at once divine and elemental, at times a god, an ancient giant, or a mountain.

In their typographical forms the characters become a collective Dublin; this complex personification becomes the logical next step for an author obsessed with the city of his birth. His wife lends her namesake to the book's central section, *Anna Livia Plurabelle*, meant to be the River Liffey and also possessing a more universal symbolic resonance—the river running into the sea as the coming of death, as well as a return to life. (The very title captures this dual sense, which is why Joyce insisted no apostrophe be used in the title. The book is at once about Finnegan's funeral (or "funferall" as Joyce punningly calls it) and the Finnegan family awaking, rising again into life. Joyce found a structural guide in the cyclical historical theories of the philosopher Vico, and he reflects this circularity at the syntactic level by beginning and ending the book in the middle of the same sentence. To appreciate fully the radical style of Joyce's last novel, even from the perspective of *Ulysses*, consider the conclusion to *Anna Livia Plurabelle*, the most melodic and distinguished section:

> Can't hear with the waters of. The chittering waters of. Flittering bats, fieldmice bawk talk. Ho! Are you not gone ahome? What Thom Malone? Can't hear with bawk of bats, all thim liffeying waters of. Ho, talk save us! My foos won't

moos. I feel as old as yonder elm. A tale told of Shaun or
Shem? All Livia's daughtersons. Dark hawks hear us. Night!
Night! My ho head halls. I feel as heavy as yonder stone. Tell
me of John or Shaun? Who were Shem and Shaun the living
sons or daughters of? Night now! Tell me, tell me, tell me,
elm! Night night! Telmetale of stem or stone. Beside the
rivering waters of, hitherand thithering waters of. Night!

Most obvious perhaps is the intense concentration on word sounds
and varying repetition, at the expense of a transparent narrative. Several
translators of the *Wake* have spoken of consultations with Joyce where he
favored faithfulness to sound and rhythm, worrying less about words
corresponding in their meanings.

This technique of course was not new to Joyce; the critic Michael
Hollington speaks of verbal association as the "staple diet of all the
narrative voices of *Ulysses*." The scholarly discipline of philology, or the
history of language, had come of age in the later nineteenth century.
One proponent spoke of a single word "having stores of poetical thought
and imagery laid up in it," and Joyce, always sensitive to the effects of
Ireland's political subjugation on its language, had long been interested
in these linguistic storehouses. In a typical 1928 explanatory letter to
Weaver, he points out puns in Norwegian, German, Old English, Latin,
Italian, French, Polish, and German. Weaver, however politely, was less
than impressed with her beneficiary's "Wholesale Safety Pun Factory."
Declan Kiberd, another critic, believes Joyce's deteriorating vision led to
an increased substitution of a "sentient ear for an imperial eye," resulting
in what Joyce himself called "a jetsam litterage of convolvuli of times lost
or strayed, of lands derelict and of tongues laggin' too." More directly,
he told one friend "I'm at the end of English."

He thus looked toward a multi-lingual subconsciousness in the
Wake, or more precisely, a *pre*-linguistic language, a magical idiom
befitting an "illuminated dreambook." Joyce regarded *The Book of Kells*,
that great Irish masterpiece, as a major influence on his latest work. In
Finnegans Wake, however, he says the much earlier book was influenced
by *his* novel. This creative anachronism is strangely consistent, for Joyce
wished for a return to origins. The Irish writer Seamus Deane calls the
book "a stupendous act of retrospective translation," a technique mainly
intent on repossessing "originary speech."

Joyce's own sense of his new artistic endeavor was more mysterious, less certain. "It is like a mountain that I tunnel into from every direction," he said, describing the challenge to a friend, "but I don't know what I will find." The English writer Ford Madox Ford arranged for the first excerpt from Joyce's new work to appear in the spring 1924 "Work in Progress," a literary supplement. Joyce was so taken by its title that he began calling his new novel *Work in Progress*; it would not receive its permanent name until publication in 1939. He edited proofs for another excerpt, this one in the *Criterion*, with three magnifying glasses and his son's help. Around this time Schmitz, Joyce's Triestine friend who wrote under the pseudonym Italo Svevo, published his latest novel *The Confessions of Zeno*, which Joyce praised. (He also mentioned that the long, flowing hair of Svevo's wife, Livia Schmitz, was the inspiration for the *Wake*'s river-woman Anna Livia Plurabelle; they responded with delight after an initial puzzlement.) Thanks to his friend's influence and support, Svevo enjoyed four happy years of European literary acclaim before dying in 1928.

Joyce continued to travel in Europe, vacationing or seeking further medical treatment. Wherever he went he collected new material, seizing Breton or Flemish words here and there to toss into his *Work in Progress*. He realized he was involved in a game, but one "I have learned to play in my own way." Unfortunately his longtime supporters were not finding his game amusing. His brother was particularly harsh, declaring his brother's latest chapters "the witless wandering of literature before its final extinction." He found the "the drivelling rigamorale" to be "unspeakable wearisome." Weaver worried about the "poor hapless reader" and suggested a heavily annotated edition be published. Even Pound was disillusioned, saying only divine vision or "a new cure for the clapp can possibly be worth all the circumambient peripherization."

In 1926 Joyce learned that a former acquaintance, Samuel Roth, was selling pirated copies of *Ulysses* in America, where the novel remained banned. The author quickly went on the offensive, and organized an International Protest. Roth was not prohibited from selling the book for another two years, but Joyce received some satisfaction in a multitude of artists and intellectuals (including Albert Einstein) coming to his defense. He found new support in Paris in Eugene and Maria Jolas, whose new avant-garde magazine *transition* would publish parts of the *Wake* from 1927 to 1929, and sporadically thereafter. Weaver continued to express her misgivings about his new project, which gave Joyce a "little attack of brainache." Upset, he stopped work for a time. Soon, though, Weaver's attitude toward the *Wake* softened, and she made it clear that Joyce could continue to expect her financial help.

Joyce was convinced that his "new style" was a significant literary advance, and he quoted the poet William Blake's dictum, "If the fool would persist in his folly, he would become wise." The repeated criticism hurt him, however, and he unexpectedly returned to verse writing, in part to answer his critics with more accessible work. The poem "Tilly" has some memorable qualities—the sounds of "They moo and make brute music with their hoofs" or the visual immediacy of cows with "Smoke pluming their foreheads." Pound, however, thought them *too* retrograde and dismissed them: "They belong in the Bible or the family album with the portraits." He advised against printing them, but encouragement elsewhere made Joyce think otherwise. Shakespeare and Company published the modestly-titled *Pomes Penyeach* in July 1927.

Despite the criticisms, Joyce pressed forward with his prose. He finished *Anna Livia Plurabelle* in late 1927, having included within it some 350 river names, and published it as a small book the following year. It would eventually be hailed as "one of the greatest things in English literature," but he first had to endure an attack by Wyndham Lewis. He also feared Eliot was turning against him, as his other friends had done. H. G. Wells showed more balance in writing Joyce about his "extraordinary experiment" that he feared was a "dead end."

Soon another couple entered the Joyces' lives, Stuart and Moune Gilbert. Stuart first won Joyce's attention and admiration by pointing out some mistakes in the French translation of *Ulysses*. He began working with the original translator and Larbaud, and his exhaustive notes eventually led to an influential critical study, approved by Joyce himself. Their collaborative *Ulysses* was published by Monnier in February 1929. Later in the summer *Tales Told of Shem and Shaun*, a collection of fables from the *Wake*, also appeared as a small book, which occasioned a portrait of the author by the artist Constantin Brancusi. There also appeared that summer the first organized defense of Joyce's ongoing project, with its tongue-in-cheek title *Our Exagmination round His Factification for Incamination of Work in Progress*. Joyce admitted that he had set "those twelve Marshalls" upon certain lines of research, and the best contribution came from Samuel Beckett, an austere young man newly arrived from Dublin (quickly known among Parisians as a "new Stephen Dedalus") He soon became a trusted, respected friend, which he realized when Joyce began to call him simply, "Beckett." (Joyce addressed even his closest friends in very formal terms.) Beckett began the French translation of *Anna Livia Plurabelle*. As a playwright and novelist, his fame would eventually rival that of his mentor.

Joyce had nearly completed the first and third books of the *Wake* by 1930, and during periods of fatigue he hit upon curious ways to maintain himself. One plan involved the young Irish writer James Stephens's "initiation" into the book's mysteries. Stephens promised if the original author "found it was madness to continue, in my condition, and saw no other way out, that he would devote himself heart and soul to the completion of it, that is the second part and the epilogue or fourth." Fortunately for literature Stephens's services were not ultimately required. Joyce also distracted himself by touting an Irish tenor named John Sullivan. His performances awed Joyce, who vowed that human ears would never hear that kind of voice again "until the Archangel Michael sings his grand aria in the last act." Sullivan had talent, but he hardly could live up to such praise. Joyce practically became the singer's full-time publicist and business manager, and his friends did not appreciate being bullied regularly to attend his operas.Joyce dubbed himself, Stephens, and Sullivan "The Three Irish Beauties."

Such incidents refreshed Joyce during the "enormous expense of spirit" of composing *Finnegans Wake*. Unfortunately he was less successful in maintaining his daughter Lucia, whose mental problems multiplied and grew more severe. Uncomfortable with her physical appearance, she had (unsuccessful) surgery done to correct her squint. Careers in singing, writing, and design evaded her, despite her father's secret assistance. In April 1931 the Joyces moved to London temporarily, partially to simplify matters of inheritance. Joyce and Nora were formally married under civil law on July 4, and her sister Kathleen frequently visited the family in England. This new environment aggravated Lucia's mental illness. She became perturbed by her parents' marriage and their warm welcome toward her aunt, and perhaps she was additionally bothered by her new sister-in-law Helen Fleischman, whom Giorgio had married in Paris the year before. Lucia's behavior became increasingly violent, and on Joyce's next birthday (his fiftieth) she attacked Nora, throwing a chair at her.

Joyce recognized his own abnormal psyche in his daughter's illness, and he in fact became more prone to hypochondria, insomnia, and fainting spells. His continuing eye afflictions were no doubt causes of these fits too; he faced his eleventh operation by 1930, with attendant treatments that often involved phosphorus, arsenic, and leeches. Yet Joyce also faced a new melancholy, heightened by John Joyce's death at the end of 1931 and his subsequent feelings of guilt. He had promised for eleven years to visit his father one final time, but time had run out. Even in his depression he couldn't resist language play, offering one friend a new calendar—"Moansday, Tearsday, Wailsday, Thumpsday, Frightday, Shatterday." Two months later he celebrated the birth of a grandson, baptized Stephen James Joyce (unbeknownst to the grandfather.) These two events, one of sadness and one of joy, both inform this emotional final poem, "Ecce Puer":

> A child is sleeping:
> An old man gone.
> O father forsaken,
> Forgive your son!

Joyce was comforted in his family troubles by a lengthening procession of admirers. A starstruck Russian, Paul Léopold Léon, served as his secretary for much of the next decade. To his brother he spoke of "the greatest writer of our time. And yet he is writing in a way that nobody understands or can understand." That these propositions could be placed so easily together safely explains Joyce's affection for Léon—if only everyone thought like him! More significantly, Sylvia Beach subtly orchestrated Joyce's befriending of Louis Gillet, an influential French critic at first skeptical of Paris's most notorious literary immigrant. He recalls his first meeting with Joyce as an evening "that made one long to speak every language." Joyce had also reconciled with the whipping boy of his Dublin youth, Padraic Colum, then living in Paris. Colum's outspoken wife, however, drew Joyce's testiness, emblematic of a misogynist strain that increased with age. She frankly told him that *Finnegans Wake* was outside literature, and he remarked to Colum, "Tell her it may be outside literature now, but its future is inside literature."

"I AM ONLY AN IRISH CLOWN, A GREAT JOKER AT THE UNIVERSE."

Joyce doggedly pursued his work, often with help from his young circle of talented devotees. Stuart Gilbert was correcting misprints in *Ulysses* for a fourth printing, and Joyce would sometimes dictate sections of *Finnegans Wake* to Samuel Beckett, occasionally with humorous results. Once Beckett was writing when there was a knock at the door, and Joyce said "Come in." Later mystified by the inclusion of these words, Joyce paused for a moment, then smiled: "Let it stand." He also hired a copyist to transcribe his barely legible manuscripts into large print, which he could then read for purposes of revision. His constant enlistment of supporters did have its drawbacks; his social standing in Paris suffered, with Monnier forthrightly telling him he was thought spoiled, and that overwhelming praise had ruined him. Nora seconded this feeling in her inimitable way: "If God Almighty came down to earth, you'd have a job for him."

In the fall of 1933 *Ulysses* was again on trial in the United States for obscenity, but this time the outcome differed. The judge, John M. Woolsey, showed a surprising perceptivity to the text, speaking of a "somewhat tragic but very powerful commentary on the inner lives of men and women." He overturned the earlier obscenity charge on December 6, and Paul Léon soon issued a statement: "Mr. Joyce finds the judge to be not devoid of a sense of humour." Within minutes of the court decision the presses were abuzz at Random House, with whom Joyce, anticipating this outcome, had signed a lucrative contract. He did so thanks in part to Sylvia Beach, who as first publisher conceded certain literary rights to the novel. The money, though, was never enough. The Joyces undertook a drawn-out, costly move to a different apartment. (Nora said of one disappointing flat, "This place is not fit to wash a rat in.") Joyce's prodigal ways continued, and he was again drinking heavily, occasionally causing Nora to take up separate residence in a hotel. "We're going downhill fast," he admitted to Beckett, with what seemed a strange sort of glee. To the alarm of Weaver's solicitors, Joyce sold his stocks at low prices for quick money. This literary genius would soon have to consider giving English lessons again.

His most considerable expense, and certainly his greatest sorrow, continued to be Lucia's advancing neurosis. He obsessed himself with her condition and care, laying aside his work on *Wake* for long stretches. (Ellman suggests that guilt drove this uncharacteristic priority, Nora having suffered her whole life for the sake of her father's commitment to his art.) Yet his fondness for his daughter made him a foolish therapist. Lucia once bluntly said she was "sex-starved," and her infatuations—a serious one involved Beckett—heightened her mental problems. Léon, with Joyce's encouragement, pushed his brother into courting her. The pair were briefly engaged before Lucia fell into a catatonic state. Consultations, clinics, injections (including bovine serum), and operations followed, but to no avail. Marie Jolas, now living near Zurich, offered to watch her, which she did briefly. And Joyce tried more indulgent cures: he spent 4,000 francs on a fur coat, and later paid to have *A Chaucer ABC* privately published, featuring Lucia's curious alphabet designs. (He encouraged her work thus "to persuade her that her whole past has not been a failure.") Any friend who failed to purchase a copy was cut off.

But far from improving Lucia, these attempts seemed to irritate her. She became increasingly violent, and in 1934 she attacked Nora again (again on her father's birthday). Her parents saw no choice but to admit her to a sanitarium. "Let us forget money troubles and black thoughts," Joyce wrote to her affectionately. He did not want to confront the extent of Lucia's troubles, choosing instead to see her as misunderstood or displaying the typical emotional whirlwinds with which every female struggles. So he remained light-hearted toward his daughter, even when she crazily spoke of writing the pope. "Be careful of your grammar," he responded in mock admonition. "He is a learned man." Lucia was transferred to a mental asylum in Zurich, and soon Joyce was desperate enough to seek the help of Jung, whom he still disliked. She had seen more than twenty doctors at this point. The therapy had little effect, though Jung also noticed similarities between father and daughter's minds. They were like two people going to the bottom of the river, he said, one falling and the other diving.

In 1935 Weaver, that suffering saint, invited Lucia to stay with her in London. This visit allowed Joyce to resume his "big long wide high deep dense prosework." But Lucia soon regressed. She said she was going to Ireland to reconcile the country to her father's genius, a prospect that must have made Joyce nervous, however much he appreciated her sentiment. Her letters turned darker, talking of suicide and her funeral, and this in turn depressed her father. "People talk of my influence on my daughter," he told Marie Jolas, "but what about her influence on me?" He convinced his sympathetic friend to cross the Channel to check on her. Giorgio and his wife had traveled to America, where he was pursuing a singing career, including a stint on NBC. Joyce became forlorn, telling Weaver he felt like an animal struck in the skull with a mallet. He could see only a dark wall or a precipice, he confided to Léon, "physically, morally, materially."

Lucia became so unmanageable in England that she needed to be committed, but Joyce refused to certify her as of unsound mind, for he did not wish to give his daughter over to the English. He arranged her return and placed her in a clinic nearby. The Joyces managed as a pleasant interlude a three-week trip to Copenhagen, which Joyce— recalling his hero-worship of Ibsen and visiting Hamlet's castle at Elsinore—enjoyed immensely. He was encouraged by the pending publication of *Ulysses* in England (he was their conqueror, he said), as much as he was troubled by the escalating military conflict throughout Europe. He expressed skepticism toward Hitler, and criticized the Fascist stances of his old friends Pound and Lewis. Instead of bombing Spain, he reasoned, isn't it better to make a great joke, as he was doing? His "great joke," the *Wake*, continued to progress, despite the trials of the author's personal life, and he often worked for 16 hours straight, late into the night. "It is a wonderful experience to live with a book.... Since 1922 my book has been a greater reality for me than reality." He informed Beckett of a discovery: he could do anything with language that he wanted.

"Knock knock. War's where!" The punning line in *Finnegans Wake* signaled the conflict looming over the Continent. Joyce traveled to Zurich in the fall of 1936 to meet Stanislaus, but he was irritated at his brother's excessive attention to politics. It proved to be the brothers' last meeting. Joyce did his best to retain his cherished political apathy, but the times were against him: by 1938 even he participated in admirable "activism," helping Jews escape the Nazis to Ireland and America. (Among those he helped was the important novelist Hermann Broch.)

That autumn he disdainfully followed England's concessions to Germany at Munich and completed the final monologue of his "monster" book. "Soft morning, city! Lsp! I am leafy speafing," the passage begins, and the lyrical life Joyce created there left little in the author himself. On November 13, 1938, *Finnegans Wake* was finished. "I felt so completely exhausted, as if all the blood had run out of my brain," Joyce explained to Eugene Jolas. "I sat for a long while on a street bench, unable to move." The publisher, Faber & Faber, aware of Joyce's birthday superstitions, prudently delivered the first copies of *Wake* on Jan. 30, 1939. Faber and the Viking Press (the American publishing firm Huebsch had joined) jointly released the book on May 4.

The publication date was earlier than originally planned, but Joyce was sensitive to greater matters. They had better hurry, he said, because war is going to break out "and nobody will be reading my book any more." (Hitler had seized Czechoslovakia on March 15.) Joyce avidly read the reviews of the *Wake* as they appeared, but most made him unhappy. One particularly pleased him, coming from the most unlikely of sources. His Irish friend-foe Gogarty called it the "most colossal leg pull in literature" and praised its author's "indomitable spirit." Joyce said the athletic Gogarty valued him for being a "stayer." By midsummer he was reading the draft of his "authorized" biography prepared by Herbert Gorman. This previous victim of censorship fully reserved the right to edit Gorman's work now that his life was the subject.

War was all but inevitable by August 1939, which caused Joyce to worry greatly about Lucia's future location. He was assured that the entire sanitorium was to be relocated to the safer region of Brittany. Joyce and Nora went there to await their daughter, but these efforts were frustrated when the relocation failed to occur. While there, however, Joyce experienced one of the most thrilling moments of his later years. One night he was at a restaurant where larger and larger numbers of British and French soldiers began to congregate. Soon they were singing the patriotic anthem "Marseillaise," and one group of soldiers, hearing Joyce's distinctive voice, lifted him onto a table. He led the entire restaurant in an encore. A doctor in that audience would later recall an "exhibition of one man dominating and thrilling a whole audience." As a little boy Joyce sang with his family at the Bray boat club, and he impressed his beloved young Nora by singing Yeats's "Down by the Salley Gardens." A lifelong fan of opera whose wife wished he had chosen a singing career, he enjoyed his most triumphant performance near the end of his life, with Europe balanced on a scale. France declared war on Sept. 3, 1939.

Lucia eventually arrived in Brittany, but another crisis precipitated the Joyces' return to Paris. Helen, Giorgio's wife, had earlier suffered a mental breakdown requiring hospitalization, and she was now nearing a relapse. Arguments abounded about Helen's being sent to America, the fate of the couple's marriage, and other matters. Joyce expectedly sided with his son, whose behavior Paul Léon found culpable. This difference led to a bitter break in the writer's and secretary's friendship. Maria Jolas, Joyce's frequent guardian angel during these final years, rescued him again. For the holidays she conveyed the family to Saint-Gérand, near Vichy, where she already had Stephen, Joyce's grandson, in her care at a nearby school for refugee children. Festivities occurred but were marred by a general feeling of somber weariness. "Come on then," Joyce said to Maria, "you know very well that it's the last Christmas."

The next few months passed uneventfully. Stephen would sit on a bed and listen to his grandfather, clad in a dressing gown, tell stories about *Ulysses*. When asked if he were writing, Joyce joked that he was revising *Finnegans Wake* by "adding commas." More seriously he said he wished to write something "very simple and very short." On June 14, 1940, Paris fell to the Germans. George arrived safely, having fled the city just in time, and Léon made it too, arriving in a cart pulled by a small donkey. The latter soon reconciled with Joyce, and they spent afternoons correcting misprints in the *Wake*. Léon stubbornly returned to Paris, and was able to salvage some of the Joyces' belongings. Eventually he was arrested, dying at the hands of the Nazis in 1942.

Some suggested that Joyce escape the Continent, but airplanes scared him only slightly less than America. He refused, and perhaps could not have made the voyage anyway; he was growing increasingly frail and regularly suffered from severe stomach cramps. Maria was also in danger of arrest, and her husband urgently beckoned her to the United States. The family needed to move on, but to where? Remembering his last war-time exile, Joyce decided upon Zurich. Thus began their exhausting leaps over bureaucratic hurdles. With the help of influential Swiss friends, Joyce arranged for Lucia's transport and applied for Swiss visas. He was at first refused and declared Jewish, a mistake that Leopold Bloom's creator would have relished in less grave circumstances. The visa was finally granted, and Louis Gillet arrived in Saint-Gérand to expedite the family's exit from France.

The Vichy government was instituting new requirements and passes on a daily basis, so the threat of arrest still loomed. However, on December 14 they made a dramatic departure, catching a train at 3 a.m.

Soon they were safely settled in Zurich. Joyce often spent afternoons with his grandson, walking along the city's snowswept streets. He didn't worry so much about writing, though he was keen to learn of any new wartime expressions, which he recorded in a notebook. The past Christmas in France wasn't the last after all, and on January 7, 1941, Joyce learned that his brother had been deported to Florence. He sent a postcard listing a group of people who might be of help. His stomach cramps returned a few nights later, becoming so painful that a doctor was called and morphine given. The next day he was moved by ambulance "writhing like a fish" and underwent an operation that morning. The procedure seemed successful; he briefly regained his strength before it left him for good. He received transfusions and, slipping in and out of a coma, asked that Nora's bed be placed next to his. His family was instead encouraged to go home. Joyce died at 2:15 a.m. on January 13, 1941. Asked by a priest about a religious service, Nora made her first widow's act a faithful one, saying she couldn't do that to Jim. She would live another ten years. Recalling most Joyce's wild life and great attention to words, she treasured a parchment manuscript of *Chamber Music*—a Christmas gift he had sent her from Dublin in 1909—for the rest of her life. At her husband's grave lay a green wreath inwoven with a lyre, a fitting symbol to honor the most poetic of Irish novelists.

Epilogue: "Given! A way a lone
a last loved a long the"

"Life is neither good nor bad; it is original." So writes Italo Svevo in his final novel, *The Confessions of Zeno*. His observation provides a suitable coda for his friend, James Joyce. "Joyce we know best, and least," delcares the critic Hugh Kenner in his study of high Modernist writers. Perhaps the originality of Joyce's life makes such a paradoxical conclusion inevitable. Aside from the sheer pleasure taken in a life lived originally, an awareness of Joyce's life permits a much more important pleasure—an essential purchase in the ageless literary works he left behind. "Art is not an escape from life," he writes in his earliest novel, *Stephen Hero*. "It's just the very opposite." Let the priest dangle a "mechanical heaven" before the public. The artist instead "affirms out of the fulness of his own life...."

Joyce's existence was largely one of exile, and the various hiatuses among his lifelong flights—his urban landings—dictated the stages of his life and the development of his literary career. For all this, though, he remained the most obsessively Irish writer: his absence from his birthplace spurred the imagination that first formed there. He was said to avoid a return because he feared for his life on Irish soil, feared becoming the literary equivalent of his fallen hero, Parnell. The real risk was likely more terrifying. "Why not go back to Dublin?" he replied to a friend Philippe Soupault once. "It would prevent me from writing about Dublin."

Of his four major works, the first two, *Dubliners* and *A Portrait of the Artist as a Young Man* are replete with the "sob of turf" where he spent his Dublin youth. Joyce's brother Stanislaus was begrudging in his praise of *Ulysses*, and brutally frank in his criticisms: "I suppose 'Circe' will stand as the most horrible thing in literature, unless you have something on your chest still worse than this." But he did acknowledge the book's main achievement. "Dublin is spread out before the reader," he said, further commending Joyce's unlimited adaptability of style. Its linguistic difficulty and dream-like atmosphere might suggest that *Finnegans Wake* is impermeable to such a local presence. Edna O'Brien believes otherwise, insisting that "oure eryan" modulates even his latest writing: "If Ireland thought she had a defector in James Joyce, she was greatly mistaken. Her music, poetry and 'broken heaventalk' are all there."

In 1999, amidst a frenzy of "end-of-the-century" lists, the Modern Library (an American series of classic works) judged Joyce's *Ulysses* the greatest novel of the twentieth century. Joyce no doubt would have found the decision pleasing—and proper. Yet the author seemed most proud of his book when it was identified in somewhat humbler terms. Despite the virtuosity of its stylistic modes and the classical erudition of its intricate structural parallels, *Ulysses* he thought first and foremost a "human comedy." This more tender register is present in a touching note to Nora, attached to that parchment manuscript of poems. With a prescience that he must have often questioned then, he wonders if this slight book will outlive them both, imagining their children's children turning its pages:

> Nothing will remain then, dearest, of our poor human
> passion-driven bodies and who can say where the souls that

looked on each other through their eyes will then be. I would pray that my soul be scattered in the wind if God would but let me blow softly for ever about one strange lonely dark-blue rain-drenched flower in a wild hedge at Aughrim or Oranmore.

SUSAN V. SCAFF

The Work of James Joyce

To read James Joyce is to enter into the colorful life of Dublin in the early twentieth century while at the same time savoring Joyce's revolutionary style and elaborate erudition. From his well known early work *Dubliners*, a collection of short stories, through his novella *A Portrait of the Artist as a Young Man* and his monumental modernist novels *Ulysses* and *Finnegans Wake*, Joyce constructs his tales of common Irish folk in increasingly experimental and poetic prose. Joyce, indeed, is the quintessential Irishman, raised in Dublin and fascinated by its inhabitants and locales. Living by choice in "exile" on the continent for most of his adult life, he draws his local pictures from afar; and after *Dubliners* he embeds the concrete details of Irish life in a radical new form of writing. Joyce's stream-of-consciousness style draws us into both the innermost recesses of the human mind and the broadest reaches of the western heritage—myth, theology, philosophy, aesthetics, literature, language, history. The richness of Joyce lies in this remarkable fusion of the tangible with the intangible, the graphically physical with sophisticated learning and the life of the mind.

Certain themes run through the Joyce opus. Joyce develops the theme of paralysis as early as *Dubliners*, describing scenes of fright, reticence, immobility and passive retreat into the safety of home and family. Joyce's central question for his disenchanted characters becomes, how do we revive and renew ourselves, whether in our family or our religious lives or in the grander theater of history? Do we take flight?

Do we challenge the expectations imposed by parents, nation and religion? Do we indulge our fantasies? Can we break new boundaries? Joyce probes these questions in several life spheres. Inevitably the Catholic Church left its mark on the Irishman, its rigid mores producing in him an instinct to flee. Just as powerful is the influence of the nationalist movement seeking Irish freedom from British rule. Art figures centrally in Joyce's thinking as well, a creative outlet that provides a way to nurture oneself and grow spiritually. Equally important is Joyce's absorption in family life. Son in a large, chaotic and impoverished household, he experienced his early years fundamentally through his family, and he writes about the relations of man and wife, parent and child, family members and others in the community.

Joyce begins his treatment of these themes in traditional narrative prose. The first sentence of *Dubliners* reflects this unadorned approach: "There was no hope for him this time: it was the third stroke," the young narrator of "The Sisters" observes, signaling the death of his friend Father Flynn (9). The sentence is straightforward, giving information at the same time that it arouses curiosity. Yet within *Dubliners* Joyce also displays his evolving dexterity with language and penchant for depth and complexity. In the last sentence of the last story, "The Dead," Gabriel painfully realizes his wife's inattention in his moment of passionate desire: "His soul swooned slowly as he heard the snow falling faintly through the universe and faintly falling, like the descent of their last end, upon all the living and the dead" (224). The enigma of the sentence lies in the meaning of "their." Is Gabriel referring to the snowflakes, or to his wife Gretta and her former lover Michael and perhaps to himself as well, or to "all the living and the dead"? The line suspends rational thought and the linear development of a single idea. It comprises a moment of penetrating yet elusive insight.

After *Dubliners* Joyce explores the deep psyche in ever more radical ways. Joyce lived during the time of the pioneering psychoanalyst Sigmund Freud. Until the twentieth century most authors took their task for granted: to introduce characters and develop a plot in chronological order, generally through an omniscient narrator. But by 1900, a turning point in cultural history with Freud's publication of *The Interpretation of Dreams*, Joseph Conrad, for example, was experimenting with disruption of chronology by using flashbacks and forwards for the reader to piece together, much in the way Freud reconstructed a patient's life story from dream and other scattered psychic elements. It was an era when writers and intellectuals were searching for meaning below the surface of human emotions and exploring the mysteries of mental life. Joyce pushes this tendency far, delving deep to reveal the hidden conflicts and knowledge of his characters.

In *A Portrait* Joyce follows the shifting thought patterns of Stephen Dedalus, modulating the style from the early impressions of the young child to Stephen's pompous talk at university to sample entries in Stephen's diary. Through all of these shifts, in contrast to such predecessors as Fielding or Dickens, he records the flow of the hero's mind. Early in the book when Stephen overhears his schoolmates talking about the boys caught "smugging" with no notion that this means making homosexual advances, he mistakenly takes the remark as a joke. Then his mind wanders, first to one of the boys, Simon Moonan, who wears nice clothes and once showed Stephen "a ball of creamy sweets," then to another boy, Boyle, who once remarked that an elephant has two tuskers rather than two tusks (42-3). What are the associations in Stephen's mind? Perhaps the color of the creamy sweets makes him think of elephant tusks? Or has something funny sparked these memories from the tone of the smugging "joke"? Logical links are missing here, and we are left to track the baffling movement of Stephen's thoughts, as irregular as our own.

It is in *Ulysses* that Joyce fully develops the stream-of-consciousness style, also called interior monologue. To record the "stream of consciousness" is to take down the roving of the mind. Written in fragments and linked by free association, the stream-of-consciousness style presents the contents of the subject's mind in process. The effect is direct representation of the mind's flow. In fact, early commentators believed that in *Ulysses* Joyce eradicated the narrator, turning storytelling into drama of the moment. However, more sophisticated analysis, for example that of Hugh Kenner, reveals minimally two levels of narration—the verbal thoughts of the subject interspersed with the subject's perceptions rendered by the narrator in bits and pieces (passim). The reader is thus drawn away from the objective external world into the character's inner self so that the text, with its irrational associations and disruptions, may appear haphazard and incoherent. In the stream-of-consciousness style the author puts feelings, impressions and sensations into words along with snippets of verbal thought, attempting to grasp the whole of the character's consciousness in its flow.

Ulysses is set in Dublin, Ireland on a single day, June 16, 1904, called "Bloomsday" by Joyce's readers. The story is about Stephen Dedalus, a young poet, and Leopold Bloom, a middle-aged Dubliner married to Molly Bloom. Bloom is in the advertising business, and Molly, who grew up in Spain, is a singer about to go on concert tour. Having lost a son, Rudy, in his infancy, the Blooms are left with a teenaged daughter, Milly, and many marriage problems, not the least of which is their abstinence since the loss of their son and Molly's pending affair with her concert manager, Blazes Boylan. Stephen Dedalus comes from a large and poor Catholic family. The story of Stephen's childhood is told in the semi-autobiographical *A Portrait of the Artist as a Young Man*, and at the end of that book Stephen, like Joyce, takes himself into "exile" abroad to become a writer. The paths of Bloom and Dedalus eventually cross in *Ulysses*, and the two characters meet in a mythical reunion of "father" and "son." The final episode of the novel takes us into the mind of Molly, recording her rambling thoughts about the day, her affair, her husband and her marriage.

This plot, as the title *Ulysses* suggests, is meant to evoke Homer's *Odyssey*. Dedalus is the Telemachus figure and Bloom is Odysseus, while Molly plays the part of Penelope. The action is divided into 18 episodes loosely linked to Telemachus's search for his father and to Odysseus's adventures on his way back from the Trojan War to Ithaca to reclaim his wife, defeat her suitors and reestablish himself on the throne. With his friend Stuart Gilbert Joyce worked out a chart to help readers follow the action; on this grid each episode is given a Homeric name, a time of day, and a bodily organ, art, color, symbol, and technique. Within this tight structure Joyce grants himself the latitude to explore the potential for heroism and love and devoted family life in the modern world, exploiting all the possibilities for irony and the comic that arise from this unlikely matrix of contemporary and mythical juxtapositions.

Stylistically *Ulysses* invites readers to immerse themselves in the moods, preoccupations and fantasies of the characters. Bloom is mature and thoughtful, absorbed with his wife's infidelity, recalling his love for her and imagining outlets for his despair. Catching a glimpse of an advertisement for investment land in Palestine, he allows himself a vision of escape: "To purchase waste sandy tracts from Turkish government and plant with eucalyptus trees. Excellent for shade, fuel and construction.... Every year you get a sending of the crop. Your name entered for life as owner in the book of the union" (4.190 ff). This would be a manly flight, bringing him profit and worldly success. His wife Molly's reverie is more familiar in tone, moving through a woman's thoughts about body and clothes, past loves, the trap of her marriage, and at last a rapturous memory of the first time that she and Bloom made love: "I put my arms around him yes and drew him down to me so he could feel my breasts all perfume yes and his heart was going like mad and yes I said yes I will Yes" (18.1607 ff).

"Ineluctable modality of the visible: at least that if no more, thought through my eyes. Signatures of all things I am here to read, seaspawn and seawrack, the nearing tide, that rusty boot... coloured signs. Limits of the diaphane" (3.1 ff). Stephen's thoughts here are those of a young intellectual showing off his knowledge even to himself. As he walks on the beach, he allows his mind to play on Jakob Boehme's theory of perception. Here, as Don Gifford tells us in his annotations to *Ulysses*, Stephen contemplates Boehme's claim that a thing can be understood only through the physical signature of its spiritual opposite (44). Stephen's thoughts shift from Boehme to Aristotle, "limits of the diaphane" referring to Aristotle's theory of vision (45). Yet for all his intellectuality Stephen is no freer than Bloom and Molly trapped in their dysfunctional marriage. A would-be poet without a job, he has no real prospects for nurturing his creativity, and the episode concludes with his glance at a "silent ship" (3.505).

A fair share of the rebellion that we encounter in Joyce's work is directed at the Catholic heritage, and if Joyce mutes his cynicism, he does so by reconfiguring religion in the extra-institutional realm of myth. Animosity to things Catholic is particularly marked in Stephen Dedalus, whose rigid Jesuit schooling leaves him disillusioned and angry. Stephen's struggle with the Church begins in *A Portrait* at Christmas, his first holiday home from school. In fact, his doubt about his faith might be said to start with the argument at Christmas dinner showing his family members divided over the sanctity of the Church. For Mrs. Riordan the priests are "the Lord's anointed. They are an honour to their country." But Mr. Dedalus retorts that priests are nothing but a "tub of guts," whereupon Mrs. Dedalus remonstrates, "you should not speak that way before Stephen. It's not right," and Mrs. Riordan puts in,

Stephen will remember all his life this "language he heard against God and religion and priests in his own home" (34). Stephen is thus not the originator of his distrust of Catholic authority, but one who has seen his own family circle split over their views of sanctity.

If doubts about the priests' authority are modeled in Stephen's own home, they multiply during his school years. Stephen is flogged because the prefect does not believe he broke his glasses accidentally. Father Arnall is kind, explaining that Stephen will be excused from writing in the interim. But the punishment is cruel, and to make matters worse Stephen's "sin" is set against two others. Some boys were caught stealing the altar wine and taking money from the rector's room. When found out they ran away, but were caught. They were given a choice between being flogged and being expelled, yet Stephen is also flogged. The boys' offenses are serious and stand in contrast to the harsh repudiation of Stephen for a mere accident.

At the center of *A Portrait* Stephen hears a sermon on the topic of hell that terrifies him. Already shamed by his own adolescent sin of lust, he goes into the sermon with trepidation. Hell is described in vivid detail—its darkness, its stench, the torment of its fire. "The damned howl and scream at one another, their torture and rage intensified by the presence of beings tortured and raging like themselves" (122). At last the preacher prays that no one present ever be consigned to this horror, but this is little comfort, and Stephen emerges with legs shaking and scalp trembling. Could it be that he has sinned so much that he may not be forgiven? Yes, he fears that he has (125). In a fragile soul like Stephen's the threat of eternal punishment does damage to his religious faith and trust in the Church.

Stephen, who once took pride in his righteousness and considered the priesthood, flees Ireland, and when he does return at the call that his mother is dying, he is unrepentant. It would be so simple to accede to her wish that he pray by her bedside, but Stephen will not yield. At the beginning of *Ulysses* he is even remonstrated by his sacrilegious friend Mulligan: "You could have knelt down, damn it, Kinch, when your dying mother asked you.... There is something sinister in you" (1.91-4). Mrs. Dedalus will appear later in "Circe" in a hellish hallucination begging Stephen to repent as he fends her off. In his youthful determination Stephen violates not just the Church, but his dying mother's religious feelings, and he remains haunted by his own callousness.

Despite his adamant refusal "to serve," Stephen is too imbued with the Catholic heritage to disengage himself and, like Joyce himself, continues to occupy his mind with the intricacies of Catholic theology. Thus, recalling the wisdom of St. Thomas Aquinas as he strolls along the beach he muses: "A *lex eterna* stays about Him. Is that then the divine substance wherein Father and Son are consubstantial" (3.48-50). Here Stephen raises a point of doctrine disputed in Catholic history. Do Father, Son and Holy Ghost exist consubstantially, that is, sharing the same substance? Or as Arius, heretic of the fourth century, claimed, should consubstantiality be denied and the Father be more accurately conceived as over the Son and the Son over the Holy Spirit (3.50-2).? This theological conundrum flits into Stephen's mind later in the day too. Carousing with friends, he this time degrades the intellectual debate with a hint of bestial corruption in the Father's impregnation of Mary with the Son by means of the Holy Ghost (14.307-8). For Stephen as for Joyce, the Catholic heritage with all of its doctrinal intricacies pushes itself into consciousness with urgent questions about its legitimacy, purity and authority.

The obsession with the Catholic religion is never resolved in Joyce's writing. While Joyce cannot leave the subject alone, he continually treats Catholic lore with mockery, disdain and even blasphemy, as in the so-called "black mass" conducted in the Red Light district in "Circe." Irony and a satiric tone often mark Joyce's portrayal of the sacred. At the end of "Cyclops," the scene in which Bloom has intruded on the rowdy company of Irish rednecks in a bar, the narrator makes fun of certain biblical scenes. An outsider who is outspoken in his humanistic views, Bloom antagonizes the boisterous crowd. In the end he escapes from the bar like Odysseus from the Cyclops with a "boulder" (a cup) thrown after him. In this grand finale Bloom is jestingly apotheosized in a parody of Elijah's ascension to heaven in a chariot of fire (Kings II). The episode doubles as a satire on the transfiguration of Jesus in the moment that Moses and Elijah appear to him high on a mountain. Ranging from horror and fear to scoffing and sacrilege, Joyce's rendition of Catholic lore dominates his stories as though with a relentless presence.

In *Ulysses* and *Finnegans Wake* Joyce does mitigate the derision of religion by assimilating Catholic credo into an encompassing "humanist" myth of human life. There is irony in this gesture. In *Ulysses*

Joyce makes Bloom a tongue-and-cheek Jesus figure, preaching and living the doctrine of love even as he displays his human frailties. In *Finnegans Wake* Joyce makes the Christian belief in death and resurrection the fundamental motif. In the beginning one H.C. Earwicker, bartender, gets drunk and falls down, and the novel recounts his dreams that night after his wife puts him to bed. The story is based on a raucous ballad about Tim Finnegan, hod carrier, who falls off a ladder and is deemed dead until the end of his wake when he suddenly awakens to carry on with his life as usual. Embodying the myth of rebirth in the concrete life and inner life of a man's mind, Joyce brings the intellectuality of Catholic doctrine down to earth in a "myth" of the everyday that is both a primordial and the Christian archetype of death and rebirth.

The fall of Finnegan / Earwicker is charged with symbolic meanings. In the words of Joseph Campbell and Henry Morton Robinson:

> Finnegan's fall from the ladder is hugely symbolic: it is Lucifer's fall, Adam's fall, the setting sun that will rise again, the fall of Rome, a Wall Street crash. It is Humpty Dumpty's fall, and the fall of Newton's apple. It is the irrigating shower of spring rain that falls on seeded fields. And it is every man's daily recurring fall from grace. (5)

Overdetermined by all of these traditions and phenomena, Finnegan's fall is the mythical tale of an amorphous Humpty Dumpty that may be "put back together again." In the natural realm it refers to a world gone barren in winter and brought back to life again in the springtime. In the human realm it points to lives reintegrated with new experience and a revival of self in love. In religious terms it suggests the myriad moments of feeling inexplicably blessed after angry frustration or deep despair, the Christian myth of grace and redemption.

Joyce renders this vast myth in cyclical terms, and the cycles bear multiple meanings. The story mimics the overarching pattern of the combined Old and New Testaments—creation, fall, life of sin, God's mercy and a return to the original state of grace. Joyce reinforces this eternal pattern of return by structuring it according to the four cycles of history outlined by Enlightenment philosopher Gaimbattista Vico. The stages move from the beginnings of perception and the ordering of things through the refinement of social and conceptual structures to an era of rigidity that renders those structures brittle. At this point the world breaks apart and returns to chaos, and the historical process begins anew. In accordance with this circular conception of time, the last sentence of *Finnegans Wake* returns to the beginning: "A way a lone a last a loved a long the"; "reverrun, past Eve and Adam's, from swerve of shore to bend of bay ... back to Howth Castle and Environs" (628, 3). In *Finnegans Wake* Joyce has reconstituted the Christian story and Catholic dogma in an inclusive and beneficent cyclical myth of human life and history.

Just as powerful an influence on Joyce's consciousness as the Catholic religion is the identity of Ireland and its people, and the cause of Irish nationhood presents itself to Stephen Dedalus as a trap akin to that of the Church. The turn of the century was a time when the British colonized Ireland, despite its long-standing tradition of Catholicism, and was celebrating its Celtic roots, language and lore and the celebrity of such deliberately Irish writers as Yeats and Synge. Bound by all of its strong traditions, the Irish rejected British oppression, and the cause of Home Rule, led in the latter part of the nineteenth century by Charles Stewart Parnell, drew an adamant following. Though a member of the Protestant minority rather than Catholic, Parnell united all the factions of the liberation movement and was revered by his diverse followers. It is Parnell, in fact, who sparks the family debate about Catholic priests in *A Portrait*. To the shock of Ireland Parnell was discovered in a romantic affair with a married woman, Kitty O'Shea, and once the moral disgrace was revealed, he never recovered his reputation and authority. At the Christmas dinner table Mr. Dedalus supports Parnell and lambastes the priests who are denouncing the lost hero, while Mrs. Riordan defends the priests but not Parnell. Mr. Casey sides with Mr. Dedalus, and Mrs. Dedalus refrains from committing herself on the sensitive topic of Parnell.

Joyce himself supported the movement for Irish independence, but believed that Parnell had gone too far in insisting upon a parliamentary form of government. He favored a different leader, Arthur Griffith, founder of Sinn Fein. Yet these are minor political differences within the overwrought clamoring for the nationalist cause, and overall Joyce had no patience for nationalistic fervor. He derides nationalist ideology, for example, through the rabid citizen in the "Cyclops" episode of *Ulysses*. Here in Kiernan's bar, filled with Kiernan's collection of memorabilia connected with crime, the Cyclops citizen holds forth on such urgent matters as the reinstitution of the Gaelic language, the importance of reviving Irish trade, the excessive punishment of sailors in the British Navy, and Sinn Fein. The citizen's bigotry is rampant, and gentle Leopold Bloom, having stepped in to look for Mr. Cunnigham, is out of his element in this loud group. In every way Bloom loses. Declining to drink and talking in his quiet way about love, "the opposite of hatred," Bloom is disparaged for his Jewish background and for calling himself an Irishman simply because "I was born here" (12.1485 and 1431). Tough-talking belligerence and rough handling make up Joyce's portrayal of the nationalist ideologue in "Cyclops."

Stephen Dedalus, a youthful version of Joyce, openly repudiates Irish nationalism. Stephen's mockery is colorfully captured toward the end of *A Portrait* in his disenchantment with his peasant friend Davin. Davin has learned Irish, joined the Irish league and enthralled himself with Irish myth. Yet even Davin has refused the peasant woman who tried to lure him to bed when he was out alone on the road. Davin could have been trapped by the woman Stephen describes as "a type of her race and his [Davin's] own, a batlike soul waking to the consciousness of itself in darkness and secrecy and loneliness and, through the eyes and voice and gesture of a woman without guile, calling the stranger to her bed" (183). Here the Irish soul is conceived as a mysterious pre-rational source of danger. Stephen denies Davin's entreaty to him to remain among their own people, casting aspersions not just on their supposed menacing primordial soul, but also on their weakness in adversity. The Irish allowed the English to conquer them and force a foreign language on them, he argues, and he sees no point in fighting for the freedom of such a lot. He will flee to foreign soil instead to liberate himself from the temptation to Irishness.

Nevertheless, like most outraged rebels, Stephen does not hold the line absolutely. A certain fascination and fierce loyalty underlie his resistance, no doubt reflective of Joyce's own profound ambivalence toward Ireland. Resigning from his teaching job, he agrees to an errand on behalf of the homeland requested by Headmaster Deasy. Stephen will see to it that Deasy's letter on hoof and mouth disease, believed by Deasy to be a threat to the health of Irish cows, will be published in the newspaper. He takes this on despite his repugnance at Deasy's pro-

Gaelic, anti-Semitic diatribe (2.320 and 413). Stephen, moreover, finding himself outside the newspaper office near Nelson's pillar, takes inspiration to fantasize a new Irish parable. Two old Dublin women ascend the monument and though feeling giddy at the top toss out pits from the plums they have been eating to the ground below. This gesture represents an urge to fertilize Irish soil despite English dominance symbolized by the staunch British hero Nelson. Stephen's thoughts are sympathetically with Ireland in these moments (7.923-36 and 1010-27).

But by the end of the novel Stephen's disdain for Irishism remains firm. When he and Bloom sit down for coffee late at night in the cabman's shelter, the "Eumaeus" episode, Bloom, advising Stephen as a father would a son, encourages him to make his country proud. Stephen's education is superlative. He has every opportunity to use his talents as a writer, and if he writes for newspapers, that is an important occupation worthy of Ireland: "You have every bit as much right to live by your pen in pursuit of your philosophy as the peasant has. What? You both belong to Ireland, the brain and the brawn. Each is equally important." Yet Stephen resists. As self-centered as always he quips, Ireland must be important "because it belongs to me," and concludes, "We can't change the country. Let us change the subject" (16.1157-71).

Pressured to obey the Church and disillusioned by nationalist ideology, where might a young man turn to discover himself and maintain his integrity? In the world of James Joyce art, creativity, and the productive force provide the means to grow and fulfill oneself. Joyce's primary artist figure is Stephen Dedalus, and Stephen struggles to find his creative power. His purpose in leaving home is not just to escape his heritage, but to become an artist. Stephen has difficulty realizing his creativity, and his efforts provide Joyce with a way of exploring art as "salvation." Stephen talks about art as something sacred, with himself as its minister: "a priest of eternal imagination, transmuting the daily bread of experience into the radiant body of evergiving life" (221). The creative act usurps the act of worship for Stephen, and his purpose in life becomes that of God, to make a sacred world in his work of art. Such an accomplishment would be his salvation.

To this end, academic Stephen turns to St. Thomas Aquinas for inspiration and develops a Thomist theory of art. Art is static, having the power to arrest the mind with its vision of eternal truth (205). It possesses "wholeness," "harmony" and "radiance" (209-13). By this

Stephen means that the work is gleaned in a moment of illumination, just as God's universe may be grasped in a moment of sacred truth or epiphany. Furthermore, just as the divine cosmos is ordered and harmonious, so is the art object. Stephen explains: "You pass from point to point, led by its formal lines; you apprehend it as balanced part against part within its limits; you feel the rhythm of its structure" (212). The artist not only exerts the creative power of a god, but creates a beautifully ordered art object, mimicking God's handiwork.

This is high-flown stuff, and it does not represent Joyce's own mature view of the artist. Joyce in his youth toyed with erudite theories like Stephen's, but he knew that to be a practicing artist the maker must stay close to lived life in its concrete everydayness. Joyce does, it can be argued, formally construct the ordered whole that Stephen describes by balancing the tales of Leopold and Molly Bloom and Stephen Dedalus in a complex textual network of interrelated parts and motifs. In fact, the structure of *Ulysses* recalls the medieval world view articulated by Thomas Aquinas. The universe is a book within which objects refer to other objects, and every object refers to God, the ultimate ground of Truth. Indeed, every thing and word is completed only in its reference to God. From this perspective the tight yet inclusive structure of *Ulysses* fulfills Stephen's Thomist aesthetics. Joyce's epic novel could be said to stand as an incarnation of the universe, displaying cosmic wholeness, radiance and harmony.

But Joyce is also the grand recorder of vivid detail, whether colorful, vivacious, sobering or obscene; and he is relentlessly concrete and explicit, describing the acceptable and the unacceptable, the decent and the pornographic, for public view. Thus, along with his many mundane and fantastical thoughts throughout the day, Bloom is graphically portrayed relieving himself in the outhouse while reading *Titbits*: "He allowed his bowels to ease themselves quietly as he read, reading still patiently, that constipation of yesterday quite gone. Hope it's not too big bring on piles again. No, just right" (4.505-10). He is also depicted giving himself pleasure while sitting on the beach, aroused by Gerty McDowell as though a seasoned masturbator and voyeur (13.824). And he is derided by his wife in her late night thoughts for setting her up, as she believes, to have sex that afternoon with Boylan and begin an extra-marital affair (18.1007 ff), certainly a plausible inference for Molly given what we know of Bloom's obsession with the tryst and refusal to intervene. Stephen's dignity is also compromised. He too is shown in private moments, picking his nose and urinating behind a rock on the beach in "Proteus," blaspheming motherhood and birth with his drunken friends in "Oxen of the Sun," and carousing and collapsing in nighttown in "Circe." These are hardly details that would befit the divine and radiant whole envisioned by Aquinas and Dedalus.

Stephen's maturity as an artist, like Joyce's, will come only with the cross fertilization of his intellectual understanding and his emotional and physical sensibility. His erudition in itself renders his art vacuous and contrived. His fancy theories deprive him of the ability to portray human experience in its extent and depth. Nor should Stephen indulge himself in rapturous romantic passion, an adolescent tendency he displays in his first poem, a clichéd outpouring of feeling for a youthful object of infatuation, Emma (*A Portrait* 70-1). Powerful art, as Joyce recognizes, neither resides in mental strategy nor disintegrates into overwrought emotion. Rather, it fuses the two, tempering both in the mature union of thought and feeling.

Overeducated Stephen must thus be reborn as an actual artist, not just an intended one, and birth imagery abounds in *Ulysses*. Stephen is resistant to this painful necessity. He derides the birth process in the most inappropriate location, the maternity hospital where he and friends have gathered along with Bloom to await the delivery of Mrs. Purefoy's new baby. Stephen's bawdy talk to friends shows the utmost disrespect for Mina Purefoy in her pain, and Bloom bemoans Stephen "for that he lived riotously with those wastrels and murdered his goods with whores" (14.275-6). Stephen will certainly not nurture his creativity by squandering himself this way. His own birth to maturity, or to growing maturity, must occur before he can perform any significant act of creation equal to that of the laboring mother. Stephen's symbolic rebirth occurs after his collapse into a drunken heap outside the brothel in nighttown. Here in Bloom's vision Stephen, fetus-like, reemerges in the figure of Bloom's dead son Rudy, "changeling, kidnapped," delicately dressed in a suit and holding a book which "he reads from right to left, inaudibly, smiling, kissing the page" (15.4940 ff). Rudy reborn, the changeling Stephen may write his own book to be read from right to left or left to right, a testimony of his creativity.

We watch Stephen depart at the end of *Ulysses* without knowing whether he will be able to make himself into a creative soul, but he now enjoys that prospect. Stephen leaves the Bloom house where Leopold has brought him from the cabman's shelter and as nurturing father encouraged him to spend the night. In fact, Bloom has also invited Stephen to become his wife's next lover, audaciously showing Stephen Molly's picture and dropping rude hints. Stephen does not stay in this new "home" and rejects the offer of nurturing wife-mother-mistress Molly. But in his contact with Leopold, and by suggestion also Molly, he has been opened up to life beyond the just plain naughty or the abstruse. For Bloom represents the whole human being, capable in his expansive personality of perversity as well as high mental understanding, but mostly just functioning as a well meaning, generous and caring human being in love with his wife and devoted to his family. Here is the engagement and love of life that could inspire Stephen's poetry. Reunited symbolically with his "parents," Leopold and Molly Bloom, Stephen might find the security and attachment in adulthood to let his own powers of creation bloom.

Whether an intellectual or a fool, artist or bartender, wife or mother or lover, Joyce's characters all bear the troubles and rewards of their lives within their families. Family relationships may of course bring about tension and misery, and Stephen at the end of *A Portrait* aims to escape his home as well as the fatherland and his church (247). Family dysfunction is everywhere to be found in Joyce's works. In Stephen's case an unruly set of siblings suffering from the effects of their father's bankruptcy pushes him to the limit of his tolerance. The noise, squalor and general bedlam of the home are too much for this young man aspiring to greatness (e.g., 162). The pressure to believe also contributes to his malaise, and the proud distance he feels from the rowdy household no doubt contributes to his resistance. By the opening of *Ulysses* Stephen has "lost" his father by ignoring him and betrayed his mother by refusing her dying wish. He has fled his family because he has determined at this point that he does not want them.

Nor does Leopold Bloom's family life offer a model for Stephen, for Leopold and Molly live with deep problems in their marriage. In this household fear has taken hold of both husband and wife. Though fascinated with each other—the thoughts of each revolve around the other throughout the day—neither can quite approach the other to request the intimacy both desire. The source of their distress is evidently the loss of infant Rudy eleven years earlier, for since that time they have never made love. The apprehension of having and losing another child may be the cause of this withdrawal, and if Bloom has set Molly up behind the scenes with Boylan, he has allowed his grief and fear to turn him into a desperately manipulative man. What does he expect? Will he enjoy Molly vicariously? Possibly he thinks the affair might divert her from his awkwardness, or he hopes that the liaison will break up his marriage since he has not been able to take the step himself. Bloom does consider leaving his wife during the course of the day, as she does him. In the case of this husband and wife, longing and devotion have combined with fear and despair to render a wholesome relationship impossible. After so many years of matrimony Leopold and Molly, unlike Odysseus and Penelope in their reunion, may love, but also dread and avoid each other.

If Molly and Leopold were able to move toward each other, they would break the stasis of their unhappy relationship. They would take initiative and assert themselves to bridge their gap in communication and reestablish physical along with emotional connection. Doing so, they would overturn Gabriel Conroy's failure to revive his marriage in "The Dead." For it was in *Dubliners* that Joyce first introduced his pervasive theme of paralysis. His purpose in these stories was to write a "moral history" of his country, focused, he said, on Dublin because the city was "the centre of paralysis." He would present this moral failing in its four life stages: "childhood, adolescence, maturity and public life" (*Selected Joyce Letters* 83). In all of these phases, it turns out, Joyce presents characters fixed in solitude or in their family relationships— those relationships most fundamental to love, life and morality.

Every character in *Dubliners* is paralyzed. Father Flynn, dead of a stroke in "The Sisters," is literally immobilized by rigor mortis. Eveline plans to flee home with her lover, but at the last moment finds flight "impossible" and, unable to move, can do no more than turn "her white face to him, passive like a helpless animal" (41). Polly drifts passively into pregnancy and allows her mother, owner of a boarding house, to set up her up in marriage with the father-boarder, an unpropitious match ("The Boarding House" 68-9). In "A Painful Case" James Duffy, solitary bachelor and lover of orderliness, is hesitantly approached by a smitten married lady, Mrs. Sinico. Duffy barely responds before firmly declining, only to read four years later of Mrs. Sinico's death in an "accident" when she stepped in front of a train. Duffy is stunned, but it is too late. Paralyzed by inner fear, he did not act in time on his attraction, and he is left hovering on the periphery of the woman's funeral: "No one wanted him; he was outcast from life's feast" (117).

Gabriel Conroy is decidedly cast out from the feast of life even though the occasion of "The Dead" is a formal dinner at which he gives a glorious speech. Of all of Joyce's "dead" figures, Gabriel is perhaps the most immobile. Writer of minor literary reviews for a conservative newspaper in Dublin, he is constrained within a middle-class society that provides no spiritual nourishment. His life has become routine and emotionally sterile and his behavior formulaic. Lost in himself, Gabriel over interprets his own importance and reputation while shutting himself off from others by talking too much and failing to listen. Only when his wife refuses him in his after-party surge of passion does he absorb what she is saying about her long lost lover, and the effect is deadening. In Gabriel Joyce has drawn the portrait of a man who is far too removed to connect in any significant way with his wife or with anyone else.

What is the hope for such a person, or for Eveline or Leopold or Molly? Joyce, as we have seen, describes all manner of entrapments and forms of flight—whether from church or nation or stultifying family ties—along with the impulse to retreat, like Eveline's back home or Duffy's to solitude or Molly's into bed or Gabriel's toward spiritual death. Art offers one path to personal salvation, but not everyone is a writer or painter, and Joyce has far more to convey about life than is illustrated by Stephen Dedalus' development as poet and author. How does one remake worn-out, burdensome relations into a meaningful life?

One answer lies in the underlying meaning of redemption, the overt theme of *Finnegans Wake* and the implicit subject of all of Joyce's writing. Certain characters like Gabriel Conroy appear to be lost, but others show movement, a sign that they are developing a personal form of creativity within their private and family lives. "Art," then, expands to become a way of life that is experimental and open to growth, and the reward of such engagement may be a break from the past, renewal of old bonds, or fulfillment in new relationships. Joyce literally moved away from the city of his birth creatively to process the components of his early life. Taking with him his lover and eventual wife, Nora, he "settled" in various foreign cities to make his own family and find his way beyond the vicious circles of his youth, though these remained his lifelong preoccupations.

Traveling this treacherous path does not always require formal exile. For Joyce and temporarily for Stephen Dedalus it is the way, but for HC Earwicker, "exile" occurs within the home and entails mystical exits and returns that expand the circle of experience. Earwicker heads up the archetypal family—father, mother, rival sons, and a daughter. Within this elastic family constellation anything is possible, from competition and rejection to fantasy and regrounding to reunion and regeneration. Thus, sons Kevin and Jerry fight to usurp their father's primacy, while daughter Isabel and mother-of-all Anna mirror each other's capacity for duplication. Isabel replicates herself in 28 like versions of the girl child, while Anna or Isabel-to-Be functions as the maternal source of life symbolized in the primordial flow of the river Liffey. Within this myth of eternal return, creativity and change are woven into the fabric of life in its negative and positive entirety.

But for the Blooms of the world, caught in the immediacy of personal crises, the attempts at a creative solution to a problem at hand generate uncertainty and apprehension. At the end of their long day Leopold and Molly contemplate the risk of giving and receiving. Accustomed to bringing Molly her breakfast in bed, Leopold asks her to bring him his breakfast the next morning. Caught off guard and unsure of the consequences, Molly ponders his request and decides to do it. With this shift possibilities open up for the Blooms. They could of course back off and retreat to their fixed positions in the marriage, but they might also reacquaint themselves and fall newly in love. With this recognition of the creative force, Joyce offers his blessing on our human capacity to invest ourselves in new life, captured in Molly's recollection of hers and Leopold's first lovemaking in the last words of the novel, "Yes I will yes."

Works Cited

Campbell, Joseph, and Henry Morton Robinson. *A Skeleton Key to Finnegans Wake*. New York: Penguin, 1944, 1972.

Gifford, Don. *"Ulysses" Annotated*. Berkeley: California UP, 1988.

Joyce, James. *Dubliners*. New York: Viking, 1963 (orig.pub. 1916).

———. *Finnegans Wake*. New York: Penguin, 1967 (orig. pub. 1939).

———. *A Portrait of the Artist as a Young Man*. New York: Viking, 1962 (orig. pub. 1916).

———. *Selected Joyce Letters*. Ed. Richard Ellmann. New York: Viking, 1975.

———. *Ulysses*. New York: Vintage, 1986 (orig. pub. 1922).

Kenner, Hugh. *Joyce's Voices*. Berkeley: California UP, 1978.

Other Works on Joyce

Ellmann, Richard. *James Joyce*. New York: Oxford UP, rev. ed. 1982.

Henke, Suzette, and Elaine Unkeless, eds. *Women in Joyce*. Urbana: Illinois UP, 1982.

Herr, Cheryl. *Joyce's Anatomy of Culture*. Urbana: Illinois UP, 1986.

Mahaffey, Vicki. *Reauthorizing Joyce*. New York: Cambridge UP, 1988.

Scott, Bonnie Kime. *Joyce and Feminism*. Bloomington: Indiana UP, 1984.

Sultan, Stanley. *Eliot, Joyce and Company*. Oxford, Eng: Oxford UP, 1987.

Van Boheemen, Christine. *The Novel as Family Romance: Language, Gender, and Authority from Fielding to Joyce*. Ithaca: Cornell UP, 1987.

HUGH KENNER

Joyce and Modernism

How the big book we're facing came to get written down, moreover with undeniable narrative skill, is a question creators of fiction used not to urge us to confront. For we were to be drawn beyond the printed words into sheer illusion; yet the arranged existence of those words that drew us in remained to be accounted for. First-person narrative is especially tricky; pseudoautobiographies exist in such quantity as to imply surprising numbers of people, especially in the past two centuries, who somehow grew up to be *writers*. They include one-time writers, too, not just "novelists" engaged in a profession; for the premise of the first-person novel is a narrator with but the one story to tell, just as you could narrate your own life, or I mine. (So, since this is the writer's one book, explain how it is written so skillfully? Is "skill" perhaps to go unnoticed, to be understood as but second nature?)

Fiction does normally imply that but one story matters: this one: for instance, the one David Copperfield has to tell. It begins, "I AM BORN," and what David can report about the time and place of that event is subject to an "as I have been informed." That Dickensian drollery strikes close to what we're canvasing, how implausible it is that these written pages even exist. David fills out Chapter 1 with pages of dialogue he can't possibly have heard while still in the womb. In Chapter 2 he's recording his very earliest memories, including the night he and Peggoty

From *Approaches to Teaching Joyce's* Ulysses, eds. Kathleen McCormick and Erwin R. Steinberg. © 1993 by The Modern Language Association of America. All rights reserved. Reprinted by permission.

were sitting by the parlor fire: "I had been reading to Nurse Peggoty about crocodiles." It's remarked, by the way, that *crocodiles* is a word beyond Nurse Peggoty's compass; she imagines a kind of vegetable and says "Crorkindills" (1, 11–16).

So how did "I" learn to read? That's not gone into, no more than how "I" have come not only to scrawl my name but to write fluent prose. (David did learn the alphabet, he does tell us later, at his mother's knee; but that doesn't explain nearly enough.) And it's notable how, ever since *Goody Two-Shoes*—a pioneer children's book and a piece of propaganda for literacy—fiction's child protagonists, well, they simply read, and they do so as easily as they walk. Thus Goody gets hold of books and is soon reading them, as though access to a book were all that mattered. Her vocation, before the tale's over, will be the teaching of reading. Curiouser and curiouser: Dr. Frankenstein's monstrous creation—a prototype graduate student, so to speak—learns English by turning the pages of *Paradise Lost*.

Yes, the explanations are unsatisfactory once attended to, and fictionists have used other devices. Lemuel Gulliver, Master Mariner, spent three years at Emmanuel College, Cambridge, and later read "the best authors" while at sea. So it's plausible that he might cover many sheets with dreary circumstantial Emmanuelese. A testy Cousin Sympson next edited the mess toward readability. He then destroyed the original, so no use our asking to inspect it. As for the script from which the printer worked, it was dropped, by arrangement with Mr. A. Pope, at the publisher's house, "in the dark, from a hackney coach," after Jonathan Swift had left England. That would gravely complicate any skeptic's effort to connect the physical evidence with Dr. Swift, whatever gossip might be alleging (xi, xiv, 3, 4).

And Abraham (Bram) Stoker achieved a ne plus ultra in 1897, when he arranged that the sole authority for *Dracula*—after, as the novel narrates, all the first-person records, the diaries, the letters, the dictaphone cylinders even, had gone up in flames—should be a pile of perfectly inscrutable typescript. Is it relevant, or not, that, like Dr. Swift, Bram Stoker (1847–1912) was a Dubliner?

Or like James Joyce? For two themes are intertwined here. One is a strange avoidance, by fictionists, of what would seem primary facts: that a written, then a printed, text somehow came into existence and that we're "reading" it. The other is what can only be described as an Irish ambivalence about writing and reading. A Dubliner named Pat Norton, so little averse to literacy that he made his living setting type, once stepped into another room, out of sight, to scan a page I had brought him. We'll be coming back to amiable Pat Norton.

"Modernism"—say 1904–90, to date it from Joyce's beginnings to the last pages of Beckett—may be described along one of its cross-sections as a coming-to-terms of printed language with print, thus with our consequent problems as readers. "Obscurity" wasn't modernism's perversity, it was virtually modernism's theme. Why anything, for instance, a voiceless page of the *Times*, is less impenetrable than it is: that is something truly obscure. Modernism has been succeeded by postmodernism and deconstruction and the cult of "text," bogeys that need not concern us just at present. And its coming is heralded when the narrator of "The Sisters," the first version of which Joyce published in the 13 August 1904 *Irish Homestead*, remembers himself as a boy, pondering the mysterious word "*paralysis*" (*Dubliners* 9), the way Peggoty, who was after all tired, didn't really ponder the still more mysterious word "*crocodiles*."

Paralysis, by the way, is a stranger word than the boy can imagine. The *lysis* is Greek for "loosening," as of muscle control; but *para*? The root means "beside," the way parallel lines lie alongside one another or a parody sits beside another poem. The *Oxford English Dictionary* adduces Greek *paraluein* and hopes to content us by muttering "to loose from beside, disable, enfeeble." The *Greek–English Lexicon* coedited (with Robert Scott) by Alice-in-Wonderland Liddell's father, Henry George, says the Greek connotes "a loosening by the side, or secretly"; hence "a breaking open illicitly," which leads to "disabling the nerves in the limbs of one side." That does still have a certain conjecturing feel. Walter W. Skeat's *Etymological Dictionary*, which commenced publication in the year of James Joyce's birth, occupied Stephen Hero "by the hour" (*Hero* 26, 30). Yes, words, a century ago, were newly mysterious, and so were attempts to explain them. Humpty-Dumpty (modeled on Dr. Liddell) had already said as much.

Less arcane, but still less penetrable, is the conversation "The Sisters" next adduces:

> —No, I wouldn't say he was exactly ... but there was something queer ... there was something uncanny about him.

I'll tell you my opinion ....
   —I have my own theory about it, he said. I think it was
one of those ... peculiar cases.... But it's hard to say....
(Dubliners 9-10)

By this time the reader is no less in the dark than the nameless boy. Suffice it further to say that readers for some ninety years have been screwing tight their attention to make out exactly what it was that mattered so much about the broken chalice, about why Father Flynn could be called "a disappointed man," about what had gone through his mind just before he was found "sitting up by himself in the dark in his confession-box, wide awake and laughing-like softly to himself" (18).

The next story is about a disturbingly sinister man, of whose ravings our boy can make nothing, though access to the word sadistic does perhaps help modern readers. But that word, not present in the story, is first recorded as late as 1892, moreover in a translation of Richard von Krafft-Ebing's Psychopathia Sexualis, not meant for general consumption. So Joyce, when he wrote "An Encounter" in 1905, seems to have envisaged a readership most of which would have access to no terms in which to think about it.

How far we are, already, from Dickens and Jane Austen! If it's an overstatement to say that the point of each Dubliners story is our inability to be sure what's been going on, still that does highlight many of the endings: the small gold coin, for instance, at the end of "Two Gallants"; the disorientation of Joe at the end of "Clay." And what of sailor "Frank" in "Eveline"? Has he really come to Dublin for a bride whom he plans to spirit away to Buenos Aires? Would you believe that, outside of pulp fiction? What, for that matter, of the sentence, late in the story, when Eveline catches a glimpse of "the black mass of the boat" (40)? What tells us that Black Mass is not a relevant phrase, tells us, too, so rapidly that we're not even conscious of discarding such an option? Was it perhaps by a parallel mechanism that Eveline overlooked the implausibility of Buenos Aires?

"People seemed [to Stephen Hero] strangely unconscious of the value of the words they used so glibly!" (Hero 26). Such a word, for instance, is grace, something gratis, freely given, as by God. And in the story called "Grace," which is about fumbling efforts to bring grace to Tom Kernan, we find the word used as follows:

> Mr Kernan was a commercial traveller of the old school
> which believed in the dignity of its calling. He had never
> been seen in the city without a silk hat of some decency and
> a pair of gaiters. By grace of these two articles of clothing, he
> said, a man could always pass muster.
>
> (*Dubliners* 153–54)

Here "dignity," "calling," "decency," "gaiters," "grace," "articles" all
open onto theological possibilities. But, "By grace of these two articles
of clothing ..."—somehow the theological gate clangs shut. Mrs.
Kernan, by the way, likes to recall her wedding day, when she left the
church "leaning on the arm of a jovial well-fed man who was dressed
smartly in a frock-coat and lavender trousers and carried a silk hat
gracefully balanced upon his other arm." Yes: "gracefully"! And "jovial"
connects her bridegroom, that day of all days, to Jove, a pagan god never
acknowledged at "the Star of the Sea Church in Sandymount" (156).

If the modernists introduced the discipline of writing English as
though it were a foreign language, they expected readers to exert a like
attention. Drafts of three *Dubliners* stories appeared in the *Irish
Homestead*, where stories were meant to be glanced at between the
advertisements for cream separators and milk pumps. Unsurprisingly,
the contracted-for series of ten got discontinued, after letters of
complaint. T. S. Eliot long afterward remarked of the early hostility to
Wordsworth, that it arose from readers who found the poems difficult
but called them silly (*Use of Poetry* 150). Complainers against "The
Sisters" or "Eveline" would have found them difficult but called them
unsettling. It was both Joyce's liability and his enablement that, unlike
his great compatriot Yeats, unlike his contemporaries Eliot and Pound,
he was not, till after he was forty, protected by any presupposition of
"art." Short stories have since come to exemplify an art form, but the
ones in *Dubliners* could be mistaken for attempts at by far the most
prevalent literary genre in those years. Not a periodical but sported its
weekly story; reflect that the *Homestead* was an agricultural journal. And
A Portrait of the Artist as a Young Man: what was that but a bungled
attempt at a book about a boy growing up, in the manner of *David
Copperfield*, of *Nicholas Nickleby*, of *Oliver Twist*? In 1916 one publisher's
reader thought it had been dashed off. It needed "time and trouble spent
on it"; needed "pruning," "pulling into shape." (Joyce had spent a mere
ten years shaping it.) (See Ellmann, *James Joyce* 402-03.)

And on the first page of *Portrait* we may be persuaded we behold modernism being invented.

> Once upon a time and a very good time it was there was a moocow coming down along the road and this moocow that was coming down along the road met a nicens little boy named baby tuckoo....

To punctuate that sentence is to destroy it. While its rhythm sustains it, it's artful too in recapturing the awareness of a child still innocent of punctuation. And "moocow," "nicens," "tuckoo": for such a child's ear those are no more neologisms than are "coming down" and "along the road" and (for that matter) "Once upon a time": as mysterious a phrase as our idiom affords.

Still, "Once upon a time" is the right way for such a story to begin, though Dickens wouldn't have seen how to work it in; *David Copperfield* commences, "Whether I shall turn out to be the hero of my own life, or whether that station will be held by anybody else...." "Station," forsooth; and the sentence wants to ring like a sixpenny Cicero. Which is not to denigrate Dickens, only to remark that he furnished what his readers and he were used to. The truth that fiction is a gestalt of words on a page was one we've seen his contemporaries evading.

But Irish Pat Norton, whom I mentioned several pages back, would have taken the opening of *Portrait* into another room for maybe an hour. Not that Joyce's Irish readers did in fact prove more perspicuous than others, though Joyce clearly trusted they would. The more scrupulous ones, though, still think print merits close attention. And Joyce did come to view his calling not as "telling a story" but as issuing instructions to printers. Put this, for instance, in italics:

> *O, the wild rose blossoms*
> *On the little green place.*
>
> (7)

Make it exist, so, in a different dimension, that of song. And hope, too, for the fit audience though few who will know that someone (mother?) is euphemizing. That last word shouldn't be "place"; no she's avoiding "grave."

And so that opening continues, all of 313 words, followed by three arrayed asterisks. And No Explanations. Joyce's first "novel" (perhaps his only novel, if you conceive of *Ulysses* as something else) is nowhere more radical than in eliminating the guide and prop of every novel-reader, the comforting narrative voice. Through the length of book after book the Narrator had been your companion, telling you the tale, supplying helpful information, making sure that you always knew where you were and when and that you were never confused. But, depending on our susceptibility to clues, it can be quite a few pages before we grasp so simple a datum as that *Portrait*'s events are set in Ireland.

The lack of a narrating guide increases the emphasis *Dubliners* places on interpretation: on the fact that reading is always an assembling of clues. How we do that is perhaps the most mysterious skill we literates possess. We've seen Joyce, age twenty-two, demonstrating (should we chance to notice) that *Black Mass* is not operative in the phrase "black mass of the boat." In *Ulysses*, commenced about 1914, this principle is extended wholesale; we can't even feel quite sure, it's been pointed out, if the first word, "Stately," is adjective or perhaps adverb. It's certain that the last word, "Yes," runs through "Stately" backward, though to notice that, we have to let "Stately" dissolve into one of the things it is, a string of letters. And—something of which Homer was innocent—"words" are blocks delimited by spaces. So we can count them. The word count of the first sentence of *Ulysses* runs to twenty-two; of the third sentence, to eleven. Eleven is the book's magic number throughout; at one point we may even find ourselves counting paragraphs, to ascertain that episode 14, which is set in a maternity hospital, sandwiches forty paragraphs (for the forty weeks of human gestation) between two blocks of eleven paragraphs each.

Not that anyone need feel constrained to count. These novelties exist on a Platonic plane, to affirm that what we confront is an arrangement of letters, of words, of paragraphs, moreover in roman and italic typeface, also small capitals, and with a sparse sprinkling of nonalphabetic signs. Such, whenever we read, whatever we read, is ultimately what we decode. And no newspaper reader is disoriented by a variousness of typefaces or by the fact that the events the paper records are united by nothing more than a common date.

The date of *Ulysses*, 16 June 1904, in a similar way does unite much indeed, including a funeral, a band concert, a footrace, a viceregal cavalcade, one adultery that we know of, the arrival of a ship from England bearing bricks, a thunderstorm, the loss of a trouser button, and on and on. Not that their date is their only commonality. There's "plot" aplenty, even good Dickensian plot, to which it's arguable that no speck, however tiny, is finally irrelevant. We've even the sturdy Victorian convention of a book that seems the sequel to a previous book; for here's the Stephen Dedalus of *Portrait*, present if not alert on this new book's first page.

But the title—well, it seems to ask us to look for Grecian heroes, who are somehow not in evidence. Still, the first nine words fall into a sturdy dactylic hexameter, and Greek words are being adduced by the second page, and soon, here's a wanderer adrift from his (faithless) wife (though Homer's Penelope was famously faithful) ... That can all be elaborated toward infinity. It remains a job, though, for the reader, the text being sparse with clues. But, throughout the Joyce canon, everything, beginning with the fate of Father Flynn, presents a job for the reader. It's perhaps a comfort to find the word *Ulysses* present four times, even if once in reference to Ulysses S. Grant.

A new novelty, though, should be noticed: extreme specificity. That is one more modernist note: small items of information. Thus, in *The Waste Land*,

> A crowd flowed over London Bridge....
> Flowed up the hill and down King William Street,
> To where Saint Mary Woolnoth kept the hours
> With a dead sound on the final stroke of nine.
>
> (62, 66–68)

—to which last line Eliot even appended a note: not a poeticism, no, "A phenomenon which I have often noticed" (n68).

David Copperfield does tell us he was born "at Blunderstone, in Suffolk, 'or thereby,'" also that it was on a Friday, at midnight (1–2). But no map discloses a Blunderstone, nor is a firm date stated. Dickens, writing in 1849, is advancing, but not by much, on an older convention that would gesture toward the year 18—, in the city of ———. It's noteworthy how fiction, the genre of the specific par excellence, tended, before Joyce, to shrink from pinning verifiable things down. Here are successive scraps from a page of *Ulysses*:

Bare clean closestools waiting in the window of William
Miller, plumber, turned back his thoughts.   (8.1045)

Against John Long's a drowsing loafer lounged in heavy
thought.   (8.1066)

Mr Bloom turned at Gray's confectioner's window of
unbought tarts and passed the reverend Thomas Connellan's
bookstore.   (8.1069)

Mr. Bloom is walking along Duke Street, toward Dawson. Miller's
was at 17 Duke, John Long's (a pub) at the Dawson Street corner, as was
Gray's confectionery; Connellan's bookstore was one shop up Dawson
past the corner ... A *Thom's Dublin Directory* of that period will verify
such minutiae. And their effect alters with time. In 1922, the year *Ulysses*
was published, many were alive who could remember 1904 Dublin; such
a reader might have experienced a hallucinatory vividness. But few such,
if any, read *Ulysses*—Dubliners were warned off the book—and their
Dublin is long since gone. Today we may settle, if we like, for the aura
of particularity, which would still work if all the details were fictitious
(thus 221-B Baker Street, the London address of Sherlock Holmes,
never existed, though Baker Street did and does). Or we can visit Dublin
and turn through *Thom's*; or we can read the findings of others who have
done those things before us: Clive Hart, for instance, Leo Knuth, Don
Gifford. We can do, in short, many things no reader of *David Copperfield*
feels an incentive to do. One way or another, a gone Dublin will take
shape in our minds, some parts as minutely mapped as Dante's cosmos.
     It's arresting that Joyce, Pound, and Eliot, the founding fathers of
modernism, were all devotees of Dante; as was Beckett, regretful closer
of modernism's gates. In a time of few (and hand-copied) books Dante
assumed you'd welcome a book that would last you all your life. In a
time of too many books (annually, thousands more) the modernists
assumed you'd welcome a book you weren't soon about to throw away.
So in the second century since Joyce's birth, as in the eighth since
Dante's, readers are busy helping one another by making lists, by
explicating phrases, by suggesting structural diagrams, by crying, "Now
wait a minute!" and threatening to bash heads. Yes, Dante would have

understood. Modernism's historians, when they arrive at clear vision, will have to take him into account.

But back to particularity. Joyce thought of it as shorthand; in an urban milieu nothing characterizes you more than your address. That Stephen's people now live in meager Cabra is a measure of their decline from the time when Stephen was born in prosperous Rathgar. Also, in the *Dubliners* story "Counterparts," Joyce moved Farrington from pub to pub—Davy Byrnes's, the Scotch House, Mulligan's—in an orbit of nicely calibrated decline. There a Dublin publisher—Maunsel & Co.—balked. Their overt objection was to the word *bloody*, though they were just then engaged in collecting J. M. Synge's Works, where *The Playboy* alone flaunts *bloody* four times. Their real taboo seems to have responded to that overt naming. Joyce declined to invent pseudonymous pubs. He offered, to no avail, to get written clearances from the pub keepers. No. *One must not name names!* An impasse. And Maunsel's printing of *Dubliners* got guillotined.

The whole episode has received too little attention. "In the year 19—, in the city of D——": that would have been the decorous way to go about it. Unlike speech, unlike even writing, print has the power to agglomerate superstitions; we still tend to call some words "unprintable," forgetting that by now the *OED*, even, prints them. Oddly, words specifying mundanities that could be verified were among those that seemed not printable. And print was Joyce's medium; more than any previous maker of fictions, he sensed a primary bond less to his reader than to his compliant printer: his disposer of italics, his omitter of bacterial quotation marks, his carefully expressive speller who should faithfully set *thaaan* with three *a*'s to designate a tune being hummed. (But two *a*'s got mislaid by a typist, and Joyce's shade had to wait for Hans Gabler's team to restore them.)

In *Ulysses*, which came to be typeset in Dijon by men innocent of the meaning of what they were setting, he indulged himself in a very orgy of what Maunsel had forbidden him, naming: not just pubs but many hundreds of places of business, even many dozen real people (one of whom, Reuben Dodd, Jr., materialized years later to sue the BBC, successfully). The penultimate episode in particular is resplendent with small facts, not failing even to let us know the name of the chief engineer of the city waterworks (in 1904 a Mr. Spencer Harty, CE).

And, "The facts in the *Cantos*," said Pound (viva voce, June 1948), "are as accurate as I could make them." The inaccuracies that have been reported make an insignificant percentage, so high is the poem's factual density. The following instructions from canto 51 pertain to tying a trout fly:

> Blue dun; number 2 in most rivers
> for dark days, when it is cold
> A starling's wing will give you the colour
> or duck widgeon, if you take feather from under the wing
> Let the body be of blue fox fur, or a water rat's
> or grey squirrel's. Take this with a portion of mohair
> and a cock's hackle for legs.

There's a joy in particulars there that works down into the very joining of consonants ("duck widgeon"). And Eliot, as far back as 1910, had adduced the "smell of steak in passageways" ("Preludes" 2), to be dismissed as "unpleasant," doubtless by such sensibilities as twitched with discomfort when Joyce named those pubs. *Aroma* would have been a nicer word than *smell*. And "passageways" ...

Information trends toward the impersonal. As the modernist novel eschewed the storyteller, so the modernist poem eschews the Bard.

And *Finnegans Wake*: if it's not dense with information, still its commentaries are, such diversities of information underlie it. By the time drafts were appearing in print, Joyce was instructing the printer not only what words to make visible but how to spell each of them. The first thing the printer must do is avoid capitalizing the first word of the first sentence. The last is to put no full stop after the last word of the last one. In between, he must by no means emend such a thing as "babalong" (103.6) to "Babylon" or "guenesis" (6.27) to "Guinness's" (else we'd lose "Genesis").

And the reader? The reader is back where the boy in "The Sisters" was, pondering impenetrabilities and omissions, getting the feel of voices, committing mysterious phrasings to memory for want (at the moment) of anything else to do with them; clutching, in fact, at alphabetic straws, all in the wavering confidence that something portentous would be making sense if the speakers, and the hidden authority beyond the speakers, weren't so tiresomely *withholding*. (They withhold, in part, because "he wouldn't understand." And it's true that he wouldn't. He'll just have to grow into it. We grow old growing into the *Wake*.)

Or: the reader is in a bar where talk courses eagerly in several languages, but it's never clear which they are. (Something about the porter being full? No, a Frenchman saying, "Comment vous portez-vous?")

Or: the reader is gazing at page after page of Text, unsure even how to pronounce the syllables, how to group them into cadences, how to do what was done so easily when *Black Mass* got discarded from "the black mass of the boat." For here it's unsure on what principle we'd be safe in discarding anything. "That's as semper as oxhousehumper" (107): are we to remember from a big dictionary that aleph was once a picture of an ox, and beth of a house, and ghimel of a camel? In which case (transposing from the Hebrew alphabet to our own), our task is as simple as ABC. And *semper* is Latin for "always," ABC's being what a printed page always (and only?) has to offer. In *which* case (we're never allowed to dodge this question): How much, ever, is our doing, how much the author's?

Yet these letters, make no mistake, are not randomly scrambled. One clue: Joyce was confident in listing copious misprints. So, apart from letters and postcards, the last thing we have from his hand is yet one more sheaf of instructions for a future printer.

But I halt at the boundaries of deconstruction, where the ghost of Priscian beckons from the shades.

ROBERT SCHOLES

In Search of James Joyce

In searching, we tend to discover what we set out to find. Stumbling upon a new continent, we may not recognize it. We are likely, in fact, to give it the name of an old one—the one we were looking for in the first place. In mental search, where we are not likely to be confronted by anything so solid and hard to explain away as a new continent, it is even more difficult to discover anything but the original object of our search. Which is why we must be very careful in designating that object.

The object of my search for James Joyce, it should be said at once, is not the Sunny Jim whose youthful gaiety brightened a peripatetic Dublin household. Nor is it the young man whose air of seedy hauteur annoyed and intimidated the literati of his native city, nor the bitter bank clerk of the Eternal City, the casual but pedantic teacher of languages, the sado-masochistic voyeur, the epistolary coprophiliac, the self-centered sponge, or the tender parent. In short, the biographical Joyce (Ellmann's Joyce, if you will) is not the one who interests me here. I acknowledge his relevance and his reality, but I am looking for another, without whom the biographical Joyce would merely be an eccentric and pathetic Irishman, like his father and some of his other relatives. I am looking for Joyce the artist and Joyce the thinker—a kind of super-Joyce, who took his sustenance from biographical figure but cannot be accounted for or understood by biography alone. The super-self of many

From *James Joyce Quarterly* 11, no. 1 (Fall 1973). © 1973 by The University of Tulsa. Reprinted by permission.

a weak and venal artist has given strength and comfort to others which the man's life may seem almost to mock. Art is one of the places where we transcend ourselves and become better than we are.

How Joyce's mind worked when he turned it to artistic questions— this is my true subject. My aim is to understand the workings of this mind so as to read Joyce's works with the fullest possible comprehension of meaning and attitude, tone and nuance. My method is not simply to give my own readings of the major works for others to admire and emulate—far from it. Rather I shall look for the roots of Joyce's way of writing in his early literary and critical productions, only partially tracing them through his later works. I shall be concerned to set his early works against their proper intellectual background, to formulate the problems they raise, to consider the solutions they offer. Ultimately, I hope to generate a view of Joyce's mind and art which will prove useful to all those who, like myself, feel that his work deserves the fullest possible comprehension.

The essay that follows is intended to be the first chapter of a work in progress that will take some time to complete. It initiates the program outlined in the above paragraph, through a consideration of some of Joyce's earliest writings and their background.

PORTRAITS AND EPIPHANIES

Clearly, James Joyce himself was always in search of the artist James Joyce. An early document attesting to this search is a brief narrative essay called "A Portrait of the Artist" that he wrote in 1904. In the first paragraph of this essay he formulated the problem of portraiture in a fashion that should prove useful in the present inquiry. It will prove useful, however, only after it has been deciphered, for it is couched in the tortured phraseology he frequently adopted in his youth, designed to impress and baffle the auditor while revealing its meaning only to those patient and dedicated enough to study each sentence and each word with care. And this, too, is significant for the present investigation. But here is the opening paragraph of that early Joycean portrait:

> The features of infancy are not commonly reproduced in the adolescent portrait for, so capricious are we, that we cannot or will not conceive the past in any other than its iron

memorial aspect. Yet the past assuredly implies a fluid succession of presents, the development of an entity of which our actual present is a phase only. Our world, again, recognises its acquaintance chiefly by the characters of beard and inches and is, for the most part, estranged from those of its members who seek through some art, by some process of the mind as yet untabulated, to liberate from the personalised lumps of matter that which is their individuating rhythm, the first or formal relation of their parts. But for such as these a portrait is not an identificative paper but rather the curve of an emotion.[1]

In this paragraph Joyce seems to be discussing both the way to make portraits and the way to look at them. He is announcing his method as a portraitist and telling us how to look at the portrait he is making. But what exactly does he tell us? Because life is a "fluid succession of presents" there is always the danger that a portraitist will capture the image of a single moment and mistake that for his subject. If he does this he acts "capriciously," trying to freeze the past in "its iron memorial aspect." Whereas a true portrait must be visionary, capturing in its image of the moment something which is not momentary but transcends time, suggesting the future and illuminating the past. The portraitist, Joyce asserts, must locate "an entity of which our actual present is a phase only." This entity which is outside of time, persisting throughout all the surface changes in a person's existence—what is it? Much of the difficulty of the passage stems from Joyce's avoiding the word "soul" in this context. The entity in question is in fact a soul-like thing, and in earlier contexts Joyce did not hesitate to call it by this name; it is Aristotle's first entelechy, the "form of forms" which, as Stephen recalls in Ulysses, persists "under everchanging forms" (U 189). A "Universal language," Stephen reflects, would render "visible not the lay sense but the first entelechy, the structural rhythm" (U 432).

The problem of self-portraiture thus becomes a test of the artist's ability to find a "universal language" which can capture the "individuating rhythm" that animates and organizes his own being. By discovering that the entity which distinguishes him from other "personalised lumps of matter" is his very ability to distinguish this entity in himself, the young man proves that he is an artist. His self-portrait doubly demonstrates his artistic nature. Joyce's continual return to self-portraiture throughout his career, from the essay we have been examining to Shem the Penman in *Finnegans Wake*, reveals him continually rediscovering the same entelechy, laying it bare more deeply and thoroughly with each treatment. As a man and an artist he had the great satisfaction of becoming more and more himself as he aged.

The problem of self-portraiture was not the only artistic problem Joyce faced in his work, but it was the central problem. And self-portraiture was closely connected in his thinking and his work with the portraiture of others and with the whole mimetic problem of representing life in art. Looking at Joyce's work as a whole it appears as if he needed an image of himself in every work as a way of verifying its reality, as a measuring gauge for the validity of his other portraits, real and imaginary. And surely the whole of Joyce's work testifies that for him the great esthetic questions were *not* the purely formal ones elucidated by Stephen in his famous disquisition on esthetics. They were not the sort of problems that could be dispatched by "dagger definitions." They had to be solved finally in concrete ways—by performance. We can best appreciate the way these problems presented themselves to Joyce, and the difficulty he had in solving them, by looking at his early critical essays and at his first serious attempt at a solution.

Joyce's youthful essays in criticism seem to have been designed mainly to impress his teachers and his peers with an exotic blend of knowing allusiveness and shocking iconoclasm. But beneath this indurated surface lurked the real problems and confusions of a young man trying to work his way out of a heritage of muddled esthetic thought bequeathed him by his nineteenth century masters—for, despite his occasional reliance on Plato, Aristotle, and Aquinas, Joyce was more deeply influenced by the English Romantics and their squabbling progeny: the Aesthetes and Naturalists. The depth of his concern—and his confusion—is apparent in his early manifesto "Drama and Life," a talk delivered to the baffled and astonished members of the University College Literary and Historical Society on 20 January 1900.

The essay, as its title suggests, is an attempt to spell out the relationship between a kind of art—"drama"—and something else called "life." A secondary purpose is the glorification of Ibsen at the expense of Shakespeare and the Greeks, and at times this secondary purpose takes over and entangles Joyce in some highly sophistic special pleading; but I propose to ignore all that and concentrate on the larger issue. Joyce begins his serious discussion by making a distinction between "drama" and "literature." The distinction is not a formal one. In a later essay, in fact; he repeats the same distinction but as between "poetry"—not drama—and "literature." This is the formulation as he presented it in "Drama and Life":

> Human society is the embodiment of changeless laws which the whimsicalities and circumstances of men and women involve and overwrap. The realm of literature is the realm of these accidental manners and humors—a spacious realm; and the true literary artist concerns himself mainly with them. Drama has to do with the underlying laws first, in all their nakedness and divine severity, and only secondarily with the motley agents who bear them out (*CW* 40).

> By drama I understand the interplay of passions to portray truth ... if a play or a work of music or a picture presents the everlasting hopes, desires, and hates of us, or deals with a symbolic presentment of our widely related nature, then it is drama (*CW* 41).

"Drama" (or poetry) is a higher kind of literature. The lower kind would seem to include most realistic fiction—which seeks to represent the surface of life in all its "accidental" aspects. The relationship of Joyce's mere "literature" to fiction becomes clearer if we look at the source of his distinction. Consider this statement:

> There is this difference between a story and a poem, that a story is a catalogue of detached facts, which have no other connection than time, place, circumstance, cause and effect; the other is the creation of actions according to the unchangeable forms of human nature as existing in the mind of the creator, which is itself the image of all other minds. The one is partial and applies only to a definite period of time and a certain combination of events which can never again recur; the other is universal and contains within itself

the germ of a relation to whatever motives or actions have place in the possible varieties of human nature.[2]

This is Shelley, in his *Defense of Poetry*—a work Joyce knew well—and the closeness of his words to Joyce's shows us just how much of a Platonic poet could be swallowed by a supposedly Aristotelian writer of fiction. Of course, Joyce did not know in 1900 when he wrote this essay that his gifts were fictional rather than dramatic or poetic (or esthetic either for that matter). Perhaps if he had known he might have found a different terminology, but he would not have repudiated the idea. It is essentially this same idea that he was reworking in that first paragraph of the 1904 "Portrait"—only in terms that owed more to Blake and Aristotle than they did to Shelley—an idea that conceives of representational possibilities in terms of an opposition between surface and symbol, matter and spirit, temporal and eternal. In "Drama and Life," however, this distinction is only a part of a larger esthetic position Joyce tried to enunciate. After separating "drama" from "literature" he went on to suggest more fully what drama should and should not be. It should reject any insistence that it be ethically instructive, Joyce maintained—unsurprisingly. And it should reject also any insistence that it be formally beautiful—a somewhat more surprising remark for a budding esthetician. Rejecting the Good and the Beautiful as necessary constituents of "drama," Joyce insisted finally that "truth has a more ascertainable and more real dominion." And truth in drama for Joyce included fidelity to the material surface of existence: "Shall we put life— real life—on the stage?" he asked (*CW* 44). And he answered,

> Still I think out of the dreary sameness of existence, a measure of dramatic life may be drawn. Even the most commonplace, the deadest among the living, may play a part in a great drama.... Life we must accept as we see it before our eyes, men and women as we meet them in the real world, not as we apprehend them in the world of faery. The great human comedy in which each has share, gives limitless scope to the true artist, to-day as yesterday and as in years gone (*CW* 45).

Well said! we are tempted to cry out, especially for an eighteen-year-old who was to write *Ulysses* in about twenty years. And yet; and yet.

Just *how* does one put "real life" into words without the result being mere literature rather than drama. "Drama and Life," like the rest of Joyce's critical writing, is silent on this crucial subject. In certain respects Joyce's essays in criticism and esthetic theory led him into a dark wood of confused terminology from which he could not estheticize his way out. But he was well nicknamed Dublin's Dante. Such problems as he could not reason his way through he solved ultimately by artistic intuition—inspiration, if you will. It is the critic's job to rationalize and render intelligible this magical process. In the pages that follow, and throughout this book, we shall be investigating the history of Joyce's responses to the problem revealed in this early essay: the problem of writing realistically without producing what Shelley called a "catalogue of detached facts, which have no other connection than time, place, circumstance, cause and effect," and what Joyce called "whimsicalities and circumstances ... accidental manners and humours." In a sense this is the problem of portraiture writ large, with Life itself, in all its fearful asymmetry, defying the artist's hand and eye.

Joyce's first important response to the problem fell short of being a satisfactory solution. It was a failure, though a very interesting one, which he took seriously for several years, and which is still very revealing for us. This imperfect solution is to be found in the theory and practice of epiphanization. We know that Joyce kept a book of epiphanies, written between 1900 and 1904, numbering over seventy. We have forty of them—enough to appraise their intent and achievement. And we have a theory of epiphany, presented as an invention of Stephen Daedalus in *Stephen Hero*. In a later chapter we will examine the epiphanies themselves in some detail. But for the moment it is necessary to consider the theory of epiphany, in relation to the concerns already revealed in "Drama and Life," and as this theory clarifies the background and the thrust of Joyce's critical thought. We must begin with a fresh look at the perhaps over-familiar passage from *Stephen Hero*, wherein Stephen conceives the idea of epiphany:

> He was passing through Eccles' St one evening, one misty evening, with all these thoughts dancing the dance of unrest in his brain when a trivial incident set him composing some ardent verses which he entitled a "Vilanelle of the Temptress." A young lady was standing on the steps of one

of those brown brick houses which seem the very incarnation
of Irish paralysis. A young gentleman was leaning on the
rusty railings of the area. Stephen as he passed on his quest
heard the following fragment of colloquy out of which he
received an impression keen enough to afflict his
sensitiveness very severely.

The Young Lady—(drawling discreetly) ... O, yes ... I was ...
at the ... cha ... pel ...

The Young Gentleman—(inaudibly) ... I ... (again
inaudibly) ... I ...

The Young Lady—(softly) ... O ... but you're ... ve ... ry ...
wick ... ed ...

This triviality made him think of collecting many such
moments together in a book of epiphanies. By an epiphany
he meant a sudden spiritual manifestation, whether in the
vulgarity of speech or of gesture or in a memorable phase of
the mind itself. He believed that it was for the man of letters
to record these epiphanies with extreme care, seeing that
they themselves are the most delicate and evanescent of
moments (*SH* 210–11).

The crucial terms here are *triviality* and *spiritual manifestation*. Together,
they unite the two apparently unreconcilable aspects of esthetic truth
that Joyce had emphasized in "Drama and Life." When Joyce insisted in
"Drama and Life" that "out of the dreary sameness of existence a
measure of dramatic life may be drawn" he was expressing a hope rather
than outlining a program or suggesting a method. But method and
program had not long to wait. They must have suggested themselves to
Joyce in much the way that he presented their occurrence to Stephen
Daedalus in the passage under consideration.

An epiphany was real, it was actual, because it was a verbatim
record of experience. But it possessed also the higher truth of dramatic
universality because it was a spiritual manifestation. What Joyce and
Stephen meant by this expression is clarified a few pages later in *Stephen
Hero*, where we find Stephen explaining to Cranly the concept of
epiphany, relating it to the three stages in esthetic apprehension which
he has derived from Aquinas. The epiphany is associated with the third
and final phase of esthetic apprehension. After the wholeness and
symmetry of the object are apprehended, its radiance becomes manifest:

—Now for the third quality. For a long time I couldn't make out what Aquinas meant. He uses a figurative word (a very unusual thing for him) but I have solved it. *Claritas* is *quidditas*. After the analysis which discovers the second quality the mind makes the only logically possible synthesis and discovers the third quality. This is the moment which I call epiphany. First we recognise that the object is *one* integral thing, then we recognise that it is an organised composite structure, a *thing* in fact: finally, when the relation of the parts is exquisite, when the parts are adjusted to the special point, we recognise that it is *that* thing which it is. Its soul, its whatness, leaps to us from the vestment of its appearance. The soul of the commonest object, the structure of which is so adjusted, seems to us radiant. The object achieves its epiphany (*SH* 213).

From this explanation we can see that by spiritual manifestation Joyce meant the revelation of the soul through the vestment of the body.

That trivial episode which first caused Stephen to conceive the idea of epiphany should now be examined more closely. It has two dimensions: setting and characters. The setting is described as the steps of "one of those brown houses which seem the very incarnation of Irish paralysis." The word "incarnation" is not used loosely here. The house is a material representation of a spiritual reality—both actual and symbolic at the same time. It gives substantial form to the soul of Irish paralysis. Similarly, the nameless young man and young lady are also incarnations which proclaim a spiritual reality: the hollow emptiness of Irish romance, in which the banal piety of every-Irish-woman ("at the … cha … pel") flirts with the flabby gallantry ("you're … ve … ry … wick … ed") of every Irishman, against a backdrop of Irish paralysis. No wonder the scene made an impression on Stephen "keen enough to afflict his sensitiveness very severely."

Joyce's idea of epiphany can be further clarified by comparison with a closely related concept presented in a work which he (like every literary young man of the time) knew well. In *The Renaissance*, Walter Pater discussed the way that certain painters seemed to select ideal moments for representation:

Now it is part of the ideality of the highest sort of dramatic poetry, that it presents us with a kind of profoundly significant and animated instants, a mere gesture, a look, a smile, perhaps—some brief and wholly concrete moment— into which, however, all the motives, all the interests and effects of a long history, have condensed themselves, and which seem to absorb past and future in an intense consciousness of the present. Such ideal instants the school of Giorgione selects, with its admirable tact, from that feverish, tumultuously coloured world of the old citizens of Venice—exquisite pauses in time, in which, arrested thus, we seem to be spectators of all the fullness of existence, and which are like some consummate extract or quintessence of life.[3]

Pater is developing here an idea drawn from the Romantic esthetic as enunciated in England by Wordsworth and Coleridge among others. Wordsworth's version of this notion lurks everywhere in his writing but is presented most explicitly in Book XII of *The Prelude* in the passage that begins (line 208):

> There are in our existence spots of time,
> That with distinct pre-eminence retain
> A renovating virtue ....

Wordsworth emphasized the "renovating virtue" of his "spots of time." They had a distinctly moral and spiritual effect on the sensitive being in whose memory they lived. And for Wordsworth, of course, these moments had a kind of religious quality because in them Nature, and the power behind Nature, spoke to the soul of the poet. They were, in Joyce's phrase, "spiritual manifestations" in a way that Joyce's own epiphanies were not, because in them a Supreme Being revealed a part of himself. A part of Joyce's problem, both in "Drama and Life" and in the theory of the epiphany, then, stems from taking over Romantic concepts from Shelley and Wordsworth without taking over their transcendental metaphysic. He wants, so to speak, his spiritual manifestations without accepting the notion of Spirit. For this reason Pater's rationalization of the romantic esthetic must have appealed to Joyce.

Pater's "ideal instants" differ from Wordsworth's "spots of time" in a number of important respects, despite the obvious similarities. In this chapter on Leonardo, for instance, Pater writes of the special moment of well-being (*bien-etre*) "which to imaginative men is a moment of invention." Here he is close to a Romantic theory of inspiration, but he alters the Romantic view by insisting that the artist's vision in these moments is simply clearer, not deeper. Pater actually speaks of a "cloudy mysticism" being "refined to a subdued and graceful mystery" in such moments. Art makes life less not more mystical for Pater. In the passage on the School of Giorgione (quoted above) he also makes it clear that what the artist captures in these "ideal instants" is not a spiritual manifestation or revelation of the supernatural, but a "consummate extract or quintessence of life." In Pater's Epicurean esthetic the consciousness of the supernatural in Nature is replaced by a heightened consciousness of the natural. In these moments the artist is inspired only to the extent that he discerns in his subject (with "admirable *tact*"), and "selects" to represent, some "gesture" in which "all the interests and effects of a long history have condensed themselves."

Pater has not only rationalized the Romantic moment of revelation, he has also humanized, urbanized, and historicized it. Giorgione and his School depict men not nature, the world of Venice rather than the Lake Country, and the condensation of "a long history" rather than a glimpse into the eternal. All of these modifications take him in Joyce's direction. But one aspect of Pater's Epicurean esthetic never satisfied Joyce. Pater praised Giorgione and the genre painters in general for rejecting the iconographical tradition, and Joyce must have accepted this praise as appropriate. What he could not accept was the value that Pater found in the work of these painters to replace the ones they rejected. Their pictures, Pater says,

> serve neither for uses of devotion, nor of allegorical or historic teaching—[they represent] little groups of real men and women, amid congruous furniture or landscape— morsels of actual life, conversation or music or play, but refined upon or idealised, till they come to seem like glimpser, of life from afar.[4]

Like Pater's Giorgione, Joyce wanted to represent an urban actuality: "real men and women" or "morsels of actual life." And he felt, like Pater, that this actuality was best caught in certain fleeting moments. Throughout his whole career, in fact, Joyce showed a preference for significant moments—scenes and portraits—over the linear arrangements which dominate most fiction. What Joyce could not accept from Pater was the notion that art "refined" and "idealised" the things that it represented. In "Drama and Life" Joyce had specifically rejected the claims upon dramatic art of both the Good and the Beautiful—singling out the latter as the more insidious of the two. Joyce's answer to "art for art's sake" was "Art is true to itself when it deals with truth" (*CW* 43–4). And he added, "Art is marred by ... mistaken insistence on its religious, its moral, its beautiful, its idealizing tendencies" (*CW* 44).

Joyce's resistance to the idealizing aspect of Pater's esthetic is a function of his adherence to the anti-esthetic esthetic of the Naturalists. Unlike Henry James, for instance, who shared many of Joyce's esthetic attitudes, Joyce accepted from the Naturalists the view that man is most himself when he is most ordinary, especially in the performance of his excremental and sexual acts, and in his abuses of the gift of language. Joyce's early acquaintance with theology helped to preserve him from the extreme naturalistic concept of a malevolent deity supervising the affairs of men with mischievous intent, and from the other aspects of simplistic determinism which informed much naturalistic fiction. But Joyce never abandoned the naturalistic concern to document accurately the actual life around us in all its trivial vulgarity. In the theory of the epiphany he made his first attempt at an artistic solution to the esthetic problem that his various concerns posed for him. In the moment of epiphany, the eternal verities would shine through the carefully documented naturalistic surface. Actual life would be recorded just as it was, but the deeper realities would manifest themselves, too, spiritually. That the spiritual values would actually be there, without any effort on the artist's part to do more than record them, Joyce seems to have taken on faith. They would be there because he *wanted* them to be there, because they *were* there. With this gaping hole in its esthetic armor, it is no wonder that the theory of epiphany did not satisfy Joyce for long. But we have not yet exhausted the resources of the theory as a revelation of Joyce's early esthetic ideas. We must return to consider further that first epiphanic moment in *Stephen Hero*.

When he first thinks of collecting such moments in a "book of epiphanies," Stephen thinks of them as being of two kinds. They are spiritual manifestations, (a) in the vulgarity of speech or of gesture, and (b) in a memorable phase of the mind itself. Stephen's own soul will reveal itself in "*memorable*" phases of his mind. The souls of others will be revealed through the "*vulgarity*" of their speech and gestures. This young man sees himself with the eye of Wordsworth and the others with the eye of Flaubert. He seems ready to write *The Prelude* and *Bouvard et Pécuchet* simultaneously.

Joyce's own "book of epiphanies" was collected largely between the delivery of his talk on "Drama and Life" and the composition of *Stephen Hero* itself, in which the theory of epiphany was set forth. The forty surviving items from the original collection (which extended to over seventy) reveal that Joyce himself had proceeded according to the method outlined in Stephen's thoughts. He collected two kinds of epiphany, which are quite distinct for the most part: they emphasize either the sensitive mind of the young artist or the vulgarity of those around him. And of course all the records of vulgarity imply the sensitivity of the recording instrument. The sensitive romantic artist in vulgar naturalistic surroundings—how much of Joyce's early subject matter is there! But just as Joyce himself had to outgrow that posture in order to become the author of his best work, the concept of epiphany had to give way to other artistic formulations in order for Joyce's best work to come into being. And just as he found it necessary to accept the sensitivity of vulgar Leopold Bloom, and the vulgarity of sensitive Stephen Dedalus, he found it necessary to reject the notion of an easy and automatic spiritual revelation which involved no more effort than jotting down his own dreams or the stupid sayings of those around him.

After 1904 Joyce kept notebooks but no book of epiphanies. And when the Stephen Dedalus of *A Portrait* presented *his* esthetic theory, the notion of epiphany was not merely absent, it was specifically rejected. In the discussion with Lynch which replaced the discussion with Cranly as the vehicle for the presentation of esthetic theory in *A Portrait*, we arrive ultimately at a moment analogous to the moment in *Stephen Hero* when *claritas*, or radiance, was explained as the achievement of epiphany:

—The connotation of the word, Stephen said, is rather vague. Aquinas uses a term which seems to be inexact. It

> baffled me for a long time. It would lead you to believe that
> he had in mind symbolism or idealism, the supreme quality
> of beauty being a light from some other world, the idea of
> which the matter is but the shadow, the reality of which it is
> but the symbol. I thought he might mean that *claritas* is the
> artistic discovery and representation of the divine purpose in
> anything or a force, of generalisation which would make the
> esthetic image a universal one, make it outshine its proper
> conditions. But that is literary talk. I understand it so. When
> you have apprehended that basket as one thing and have then
> analysed it according to its form and apprehended it as a
> thing you make the only synthesis which is logically and
> esthetically permissible. You see that it is the thing it is and
> no other thing. The radiance of which he speaks is the
> scholastic *quidditas*, the whatness of a thing (*Portrait* 212–12).

This second formulation quite specifically repudiates all the Shelleyan
idealism which animated the notion of epiphany in *Stephen Hero*. The
"symbolism" or "idealism" which Stephen and Joyce once thought of as
showing through the vestments of the commonest object is here
dismissed as mere "literary talk." This is a tougher-minded Stephen and
a tougher-minded Joyce. Any "force of generalisation" in Joyce's work
after *Stephen Hero* was to be earned by artistic effort rather than assumed
as the divine right of esthetic sensitivity.

By the time of *Ulysses* both Joyce and Stephen had attained a
distance from the Epiphanies sufficient for mockery. In Stephen's
interior monologue on Sandymount Strand they appear like an ironic
spot of time, annoying rather than refreshing, and are subject themselves
to a renovating scrutiny:

> Remember your epiphanies on green oval leaves, deeply
> deep, copies to be sent if you died to all the great libraries of
> the world, including Alexandria? Someone was to read them
> there after a few thousand years, a mahamanvantara. Pico
> della Mirandola like. Ay, very like a whale. When one reads
> these strange pages of one long gone one feels that one is at
> one with one who once ... (*U* 40).

Thus the epiphany was tried and ultimately rejected as the solution to the problems first posed in "Drama and Life." But the problems did not disappear along with the rejection of this first solution. They remained because they were the problems of the age, which is to say the age's version of the perennial problems of the artist. How to tell the truth, the deep truths about the human condition, without writing mere documentary realism—this was the problem Joyce and his contemporaries faced, and Joyce himself made the problem especially difficult and interesting by insisting that his deep truth do no violence to that shabby surface realism, that vulgarity of speech and of gesture, which he loved and hated, and learned to present with his own kind of radiance in his finest work.

NOTES

1. *The Workshop of Daedalus: James Joyce and the Materials for "A Portrait of the Artist as a Young Man,"* ed. Robert Scholes and Richard M. Kain (Evanston: Northwestern University Press, 1965), p. 60.

2. Percy Bysshe Shelley, "A Defense of Poetry," in *Shelley's Prose or the Trumpet of a Prophecy*, ed. David Lee Clark (Albuquerque: University of New Mexico Press, 1954), p. 281.

3. *The Renaissance* (1873; New York: Modern Library, n.d.), pp. 123–24.

4. *Ibid.*, p. 116.

Chronology

1882	James Augustine Joyce, the eldest child of John and May Joyce, is born on February 2 in Rathgar, near Dublin.
1884	Birth of Stanislaus Joyce, the sibling with whom he was closest.
1888	Family moves south of Dublin, Joyce enrolled in the Jesuit-run Clongowes Wood College.
1890	The political fall of Charles Parnell, which Joyce would dramatize in *Dubliners* and *A Portrait of the Artist as a Young Man*.
1891–2	Financial difficulties beset Joyce family; Joyce withdrawn from Clongowes, and family moves to Blackrock, a suburb of Dublin.
1893	Family relocates again to Dublin proper; Joyce enrolled at Belvedere College, another Jesuit school.
1897	At 15, wins academic prize for best English composition in Ireland for his grade.
1898	Enters University College, Dublin.
1899	Attends the opening performance of William Butler Yeats' *The Countess Cathleen*, an occasion marred by protests and riots.
1900	Publishes article in *The Fortnightly Review* on the Norwegian playwright Henrik Ibsen, for which he is thanked by Ibsen himself. Writes poems and plays, many of which are lost.

1901	Private publication of "The Day of the Rabblement," an essay attacking provincialism in Irish literature.
1902	Graduates from University College. In December leaves Dublin for Paris, with plans to study medicine.
1903	Learns that his mother is increasingly ill; returns to Dublin in April; mother dies on August 13.
1904	Residing at various Dublin addresses. Meets Nora Barnacle on June 10; they go out on June 16, the day immortalized in *Ulysses* and later known as Bloomsday. Joyce writes an essay, "A Portrait of the Artist," as well as poems and stories, and he begins *Stephen Hero*. Leaves for the Continent in October accompanied (unbeknownst to his family) by Nora; after rebuff by the Berlitz School in Zurich, he is given a tutoring position in Pola, Yugoslavia.
1905	Begins working for Berlitz School in Trieste. Son, Giorgio, born on July 27. Grant Richards, a London publisher, considers (and delays) printing *Chamber Music* and *Dubliners*. Stanislaus arrives in Trieste to reside with Joyce and his family.
1906	Moves to Rome, where his father helps him obtain a position as a bank clerk. Continues work on *Dubliners*.
1907	Returns to Trieste, where he tutors pupils in English and gives public lectures. Daughter, Lucia, born on July 26. *Chamber Music* published in London; begins rewriting *Stephen Hero*, dramatically altering it and shortening it into *A Portrait of the Artist as a Young Man*.
1909	Returns to Dublin, once to sign a contract for *Dubliners* and again to open a cinema; both projects shortly fail. Shaken by insinuations that Nora is unfaithful. His sister Eva returns with him to Trieste.
1912	Final trip to Dublin; battles editor about the publication of *Dubliners*. Fearing libel charges, a printer destroys the book's print sheets. Joyce, who has a second copy of the sheets, satirizes the editor by writing the poem "Gas from a Burner" on the train back to Trieste.
1913	The American poet and Modernist lightning rod Ezra Pound contacts Joyce.

1914	*Dubliners* finally published by Grant Richards, and *Portrait* begins appearing serially in the *Egoist*, a literary journal. Joyce writes *Giacomo Joyce*, begins *Ulysses*; World War I commences.
1915	Facing internment in Trieste, the Joyce family seeks neutral ground in Zurich. Joyce's play, *Exiles*, completed.
1916	*A Portrait* published in New York.
1917	Joyce undergoes first of several eye operations; receives financial help from Harriet Shaw Weaver, a life-long supporter.
1918	*Exiles* published in London; sections of *Ulysses* begin to appear in *Little Review*.
1919	War ceases, making possible a return to Trieste.
1920	The family instead relocates to Paris, at the suggestion of Pound. *Little Review* ordered by court to halt publication of *Ulysses* excerpts.
1922	*Ulysses* published in Paris by Sylvia Beach, proprietor of the bookshop Shakespeare and Company. Event coincides with Joyce's fortieth birthday.
1923	Joyce begins "Work in Progress," which is eventually released as *Finnegans Wake*.
1927	*Pomes Penyeach* published, also by Beach. "Work in Progress" begins to be published in *transition*, an avant-garde magazine.
1929	Joyce defended by the playwright (and his former secretary) Samuel Beckett and eleven others, in essays collected in *Our Exagmination round His Factification for Incamination of Work in Progress*.
1931	Joyce and Nora married in London, 27 years after they first meet. Joyce's father dies.
1932	First child born to Giorgio and Helen Joyce; this birth and the loss of Joyce's father are alternately commemorated in his short poem, "Ecce Puer." Lucia Joyce suffers a mental breakdown.
1933	U.S. Court permits publication of *Ulysses*. Lucia is treated at a Swiss hospital.
1934	*Ulysses* published by Random House in New York.

1939	*Finnegans Wake* published by Faber & Faber in London and Viking in New York. The Joyce family moves to southern France as World War II begins.
1940	Family is permitted to flee France and return to Zurich.
1941	Joyce suffers a perforated ulcer, dies on January 13 at the age of 58.
1951	Nora dies in Zurich.

Works by James Joyce

Chamber Music, 1907.

Dubliners, 1914.

A Portrait of the Artist as a Young Man, 1916.

Exiles, 1918.

Pomes Penyeach, 1927.

Ulysses, 1922.

Finnegans Wake, 1939.

Stephen Hero, 1944 (posthumous).

Epiphanies (1904–6), 1956 (posthumous).

Giacomo Joyce, 1968 (posthumous).

Letters. 3 vols., 1957, 1966.

Selected Letters, 1975. [with correspondence not printed elsewhere]

Critical Writings, 1959. Rpt. 1989.
Poems and Shorter Writings, 1991.

Works about James Joyce

Anderson, Chester G. *James Joyce and his World*. New York: Viking Press, 1968.

Brown, Malcolm. *The Politics of Irish Literature*. Seattle: University of Washington Press, 1972.

Budgen, Frank. *James Joyce and the Making of Ulysses*. Bloomington: Indiana University Press, 1960.

Eliot, T .S. "*Ulysses*, Order, and Myth." *Selected Prose of T. S. Eliot*. New York: Harcourt Brace Jovanovich, 1975.

Gilbert, Stuart. *Reflections on James Joyce*. Ed. Thomas F. Staley and Randolph Lewis. Austin: University of Texas Press, 1993.

Gregory, Lady. *Selected Writings*. London: Penguin Books, 1995.

Heaney, Seamus. *Finders Keepers*. New York: Farrar, Strauss and Giroux, 2002.

Hollington, Michael. "Svevo, Joyce, and Modernist Time." *Modernism: A Guide to European Literature 1890–1930*. Ed. Malcolm Bradury and James McFarlane. London: Penguin Books, 1976.

Johnston, Dillon. *Irish Poetry After Joyce*. Notre Dame: University of Notre Dame Press, 1985.

Joyce, Stanislaus. *My Brother's Keeper*. Ed. Richard Ellman. New York: The Viking Press, 1958.

———. *The Complete Dublin Diaries of Stanislaus Joyce*. Ithaca: Cornell University Press, 1962.

Kenner, Hugh. *The Pound Era*. Berkeley: University of California Press, 1971.

Kiberd, Declan. *Inventing Ireland: The Literature of the Modern Nation*. Cambridge: Harvard University Press, 1995.

MacNeice, Louis. *The Poetry of W. B. Yeats*. Oxford: Oxford University Press, 1941.

Maddox, Brenda. *Nora: The Real Life of Molly Bloom*. Boston: Houghton Mifflin, 1988.

O'Brien, Edna. *James Joyce*. New York: Viking Penguin, 1999.

Potts, Willard, ed. *Portraits of the Artist in Exile: Recollections of James Joyce by Europeans*. Seattle: University of Washington Press, 1979.

Power, Arthur. *Conversations with James Joyce*. Ed. Clive Hart. London: Millington, 1974.

Read, Forrest, ed. *Pound/Joyce: The Letters of Ezra Pound to James Joyce*. New York: New Directions, 1970.

Stoppard, Tom. *Travesties*. New York: Grove Press, 1975.

Van Ghent, Dorothy. *The English Novel: Form and Function*. New York: Harper & Brothers, 1961.

Contributors

HAROLD BLOOM is Sterling Professor of the Humanities at Yale University and Henry W. and Albert A. Berg Professor of English at the New York University Graduate School. He is the author of over 20 books, including *Shelley's Mythmaking* (1959), *The Visionary Company* (1961), *Blake's Apocalypse* (1963), *Yeats* (1970), *A Map of Misreading* (1975), *Kabbalah and Criticism* (1975), *Agon: Toward a Theory of Revisionism* (1982), *The American Religion* (1992), *The Western Canon* (1994), and *Omens of Millennium: The Gnosis of Angels, Dreams, and Resurrection* (1996). *The Anxiety of Influence* (1973) sets forth Professor Bloom's provocative theory of the literary relationships between the great writers and their predecessors. His most recent books include *Shakespeare: The Invention of the Human* (1998), a 1998 National Book Award finalist, *How to Read and Why* (2000), and *Genius: A Mosaic of One Hundred Exemplary Creative Minds* (2002). In 1999, Professor Bloom received the prestigious American Academy of Arts and Letters Gold Medal for Criticism, and in 2002 he received the Catalonia International Prize.

BRETT FOSTER is a Harvey Fellow in Yale University's Department of English. He has also held a Wallace Stegner Fellowship in poetry at Stanford University, where he led honors tutorials on James Joyce. His essays, poems, and translations have appeared in many literary journals, including *Agni*, *Boston Review*, *The Georgia Review*, *Harvard Review*, *The Missouri Review*, *Partisan Review*, and *Poetry International*.

SUSAN V. SCAFF is an Associate Professor of English at San Jose State University. In addition to her work on Joyce she has also published on *Jane Eyre*.

HUGH KENNER is considered one of the 20th century's preeminent scholars on modernism. His book, *The Poetry of Ezra Pound* (1951) was the first serious publication on the subject in America, and his volumes *Dublin's Joyce* (1955) and *Joyce's Voices* (1978) are standards of Joyce criticism.

ROBERT SCHOLES is Andrew W. Mellon Professor Emeritus of English, Comparative Literature and Modern Culture and Media at Brown University. In his prolific career, Professor Scholes has written extensively on modern literature and literary technique, and his most recent publications include *In Search of James Joyce* (1992) *The Rise and Fall of English* (1998) and *The Crafty Reader* (2001).

INDEX